thegoodwebguide

comedy

Dedication

For Peter and Anne.
What would I have done without you?

thegoodwebguide

comedy

Paul Chronnell

The Good Web Guide Limited • London

First Published in Great Britain in 2001 by The Good Web Guide Limited

Broadwall House, 21 Broadwall, London, SE1 9PL

www.thegoodwebguide.co.uk

Email:feedback@thegoodwebguide.co.uk

© 2001 The Good Web Guide Ltd

Text © 2001 Paul Chronnell

Original series concept by Steve Bailey.

Cover photo © Getty Images Stone

10 9 8 7 6 5 4 3 2 1

A catalogue record for this book is available from the British Library.

ISBN 1-903282-209

Project Editor Michelle Clare

Design by Myriad Creative Ltd

Printed in Italy at LEGO S.p.A.

contents

the good web guides

The World Wide Web is a vast resource, with millions of sites on every conceivable subject, where cyber-communities have grown, and people have formed relationships, and even married on the net.

However, busy people want to use the internet for quick access to information, rather than spending hours on end surfing; it can be a quick and useful resource if you are looking for specific information.

The Good Web Guides have been published with this in mind, and to give you a head start in your search, our researchers have come up with a collection of reviews of the best sites around.

Our recommendation is impartial ; reviews are focused on the website and what it sets out to do, rather than an endorsement of a company, or their product. A small but beautiful site run by a one-man band may be rated higher than an ambitious but flawed site run by a mighty organisation.

Relevance to the UK-based visitor is also given a high premium: tantalising as it is to read about purchases you can make in California, because of delivery charges, import duties and controls it may not be as useful as a local site.

Our reviewers considered a number of questions when reviewing the sites, such as: How quickly do the sites and individual pages download? Can you move around the site easily and get back to where you started, and do the links work? Is the information up to date and accurate? And is the site pleasing to the eye and easy to read? More importantly, we also asked whether the site has something distinctive to offer. On the basis of the answers to these questions, sites are given ratings out of five. As we aim only to include sites that we feel are of serious interest, there are very few low-rated sites.

Remember: the collection of reviews you see here is just a snapshot of the sites at a particular time. The process of choosing and writing about sites is rather like painting the Forth Bridge: as each section appears complete, new sites are launched and others are modified.

As this is the first edition of the Good Web Guide, all our sites have been reviewed by the author and research team, but we'd like to know what you think. Contact us via the website or email feedback@thegoodwebguide.co.uk. You are welcome to recommend sites, quibble about the ratings, point out changes and inaccuracies or suggest new features to assess.

You can find us at www.thegoodwebguide.co.uk

introduction

A recent search of the internet unearthed 1,090, 455 hits for the word Comedy. However, the word Politics got nearly three million! Laughter suggested 454,449 places of interest while Depression was rooted in 976,937 sites. And, although we can console ourselves that Armadillo received 46,059 hits to Richard Whitely's meagre 148, it is clear that the internet is leaning toward content that spoils our day by simply refusing to be entertaining and humorous. Surely the internet is awash with fun, if we just knew where to look...

I have wandered around the internet, sometimes on hands and knees, trying to find sites worthy of inclusion in this guide. And after sifting through some absolute dross, I have come to a single thought that sums up the humour content of the net, 'Subjective'. Many times I recounted a site to a friend, secure in the knowledge that the briefest of descriptions would bring a smile, if not laughter, to their face, only to be met with a worried look and the well thought out response, 'eh?'.

So don't become too upset if your very favourite humorous topics are not covered in this guide. Some of my own had to be excluded as I simply couldn't find a site good enough to warrant their inclusion. But the situation is changing all the time. New sites are popping up, old sites are being revamped in order to compete, and whole new areas of comedy, new films, books, TV programmes, comedians, ridiculous nonsense, are vying for attention and your browsing time. So, it's a good idea to check the regular updates that will be posted at www.thegoodwebguide.co.uk to make sure you don't miss out on any laughs.

Remember, this guide is about humour. Celebrating performers, actors or productions that are funny, or simply finding internet stuff to make you giggle. Get out there and enjoy the net, the world is just way too serious.

Finally, having just the one sense of humour, I am very keen to find out what sites other people think should be included in the next edition. Feel free to let me know all your views, I don't bite. And if I do feel a little 'snappy', I'll wear a muzzle.

Paul Chronnell, February 2001

acknowledgements

I would love to do a Spike Milligan and say that I didn't want to thank anyone because I did it all myself, but this would be lies. Huge thanks go to all the following.

There is absolutely no way this book would ever have been finished without the never ending support of Jorgi, Eddie and Dreyfuss, who listened patiently while I ranted and forgave me when I was horrid.

My parents have to be thanked, probably daily, for all the long phone calls, quiet reassurances and basically knowing pretty much everything about me and still quite liking me.

Huge gratitude must go to Elaine Collins from the Good Web Guide for sensibly putting me away in a file marked 'interesting' and then losing her mind, taking me out again, and asking me to write this guide. Thanks to Elaine and Michelle for answering my questions that I could never simply just ask, without the need to prattle.

Writing is a lonely business so I am indebted to all those who helped keep me sane. Adrian and Gemma for being well versed in the art of friendship, but being past masters at the art of drinking wine. Miles and Annabelle who kindly emailed help and suggestions. Phil, who made suggestions I couldn't use but never failed to be at least partially enthusiastic. Rou, who never made taking time off a problem. Mad Jane for listening to me moan without adding grumbles of her own, infecting people with her lunacy, and reminding me that life is an adventure, not a chore.

Wet sloppy kisses to all.

user key

£   subscription required

R   registration required

🔒   secure online ordering

UK   country of origin

animation

Not so long ago, when you mentioned animation, especially humorous animation, most people thought of children's cartoons and the gentle humour of an occasional Disney film. More recently, animated series have emerged, aimed at an older audience. The Simpsons and South Park are now huge industries in their own right and the internet makes room for this shift towards animation that makes you laugh out loud. A number of the sites that follow are run by individuals who have nothing but artistic talent and a strange sense of humour. They take the playful 'violence' of Tom and Jerry and add blood, death and occasionally interactivity, and a new breed of comedy is born. That's not to say there's no longer a place for the traditional style cartoon, and some of the sites in this section reflect that. And the Muppets? Yeah, we know they're not actually animation, but we couldn't have a chapter simply for naked frogs and egocentric pigs, now could we?

comedy

overall rating:	★ ★ ★ ★ ★
classification:	fan site
updated:	frequently
navigation:	★ ★ ★ ★ ★
content:	★ ★ ★ ★ ★
readability:	★ ★ ★ ★
speed:	★ ★ ★ ★
UK	

www.beef-cake.com
Beef-Cake.Com

There are a lot of South Park sites on the internet but this is one of the much better ones. It used to be three sites but now is one super-site, and it claims to carry more South Park images and sounds than any other. It's updated frequently and all the latest news can be found in the blue section which, slightly annoyingly, runs for miles up and down the main page. The latest changes are in the smaller blue box at the top of the page and the necessary navigation buttons run down the left-hand side.

SPECIAL FEATURES

News Archive If the current South Park news isn't enough for you, check out this list of newsworthy material, which stretches back to September 1999. Unusually, you also get a reminder that some of the links in the news may be broken due to other sites closing or changing.

Beef-Cake FAQ Very useful section this. Instead of miles of South Park trivia, you have everything here telling you how to get the best out of the site. There are instructions on how to download things and what to do if things don't behave as expected. Interesting and helpful.

Beef-Cake Interactive It's split up into eight subsections. We've listed the most interesting of these below.

The Message Board is actually 11 message boards with nearly 30,000 posts and counting. You have to register to get involved, but this is free and only takes a couple of minutes.

If you're feeling creative you can read one of 1,800 Haikus written by fans. A lot of these three line poems have questionable content, both in terms of talent and vulgarity.

The Chat Room is a link to the IRC server where the chat room is located. If you haven't got the right equipment to join in, there's also information on where to get it.

Last year the site asked its visitors to send in the questions they would most like to ask South Park's two creators, Matt Stone and Trey Parker. The most popular questions were asked, and in Twenty Questions you can download audio files of Matt and Trey answering them. An interesting slant on the usual Q&A format.

South Park Episodes Each episode has its own plot summary, interesting facts and figures and links to dozens of sounds; loads of images, which you can only view one at a time in a slide show; the script and a link for the acrobat reader you need to view it; and DYN's, which is a list of 'Did You Notice' things from each episode.

South Park Media This is just a simpler way of accessing the sounds, images and scripts without, as they put it, 'all the tedious mucking about in the episode section of the site'.

With so many downloads and so much information, if you can't find it here it probably doesn't exist.

comedy

overall rating: ★★★★★
classification: homepage
updated: weekly
navigation: ★★★★
content: ★★★★★
readability: ★★★★★
speed: ★★★
US

http://www.joecartoon.com
Joe Cartoon

Another graphic intensive site, one of the best, but it requires a coarse sense of humour and is not suitable for those of a delicate disposition. It rates itself as PG-13.5. Navigate by clicking the white section headings or, if you prefer a simple and uninteresting list of contents, click the Site Map icon. Everything takes a while to load but you're given silly graphics to watch while you wait. A word of warning – virtually everything on here ends with someone or something getting bashed, splatted or decapitated. You'll know in seconds whether this site is for you or whether you think it's childish nonsense. Claims to be updated once a week so it will keep you coming back for more.

SPECIAL FEATURES

New Stuff The latest cartoons to download. They can take quite a long time but they're full colour and have great sounds.

Cartoons These take slightly less time to download and have much simpler animation. If you're enjoying the comedic style so far, you'll love these too.

Classic Joe/Shoot the Singer/Micro Gerbil These are three of the most famous Joe Cartoon animations and have been doing the rounds on the internet for some time. All well worth the download time. All are interactive.

Comics A series of single frame cartoons featuring the same character or theme. Click on the arrows for the next or previous cartoons. The brand of humour is the same, but after the animations they're just not as funny.

Downloads Here are some of the best animations to download to your desktop and send to your friends. There's a choice of PC or Mac versions, and there's loads to choose from.

Greetings Cards Much more fun than the usual boring ecards.

Newsletter Sign up and be kept informed about once a month. Joe's email address is here too, if you want to complain. Be warned, though; Joe doesn't really have much respect for people who complain.

Buy Stuff Like what you've seen? So buy a T-shirt, or a mug, or even Joe Cartoon toilet paper. It's an American site but they'll ship to England. It's secure online ordering too.

Joe The Legend Find out about the man behind the madness. Entertainingly tongue-in-cheek. If it's too small to read, right click and choose 'zoom'.

Drinking Buddies The links take you to cartoons created by friends of Joe. Some of these cartoons contain strong language.

If you lost your sense of humour when you left your teens you may well find this site infantile and stupid. If not, you'll be rolling on the floor.

comedy

overall rating:	★ ★ ★ ★ ★
classification:	homepage
updated:	fortnightly
navigation:	★ ★ ★ ★ ★
content:	★ ★ ★ ★ ★
readability:	★ ★ ★ ★ ★
speed:	★ ★ ★ ★
UK	**18**

http://www.killfrog.com
Kill Frog

Kill Frog is not a site with cartoons for children, unless of course they're children who like to see gratuitous comic violence, characters like the Evil Pigs and story lines where people end up dead. That aside, it is a very funny site. The creator is a friend of Joe Cartoon (see p.16) and there are some noticeable similarities. The cartoon stories are well made, the sound and voices are excellent and the download times are better than you might expect given the amount of graphics. Even the waiting is made more interesting, as music plays and occasional 'trailers' pop up for you to enjoy. Navigation is simple, simply choose from the icons in the Remote tower on the left, and the site is updated every other week.

SPECIAL FEATURES

New Stuff This is where you can get an immediate taste for the site. It's nasty comedy but very funny. The next three features are some of the best available.

The Little Susie Experiments She's a little girl who has trouble getting to sleep, which isn't surprising as she has three little evil pigs who want to experiment with her in awful ways that always end up with both her and her cat dead; even the evil pigs don't always make it to the end. Throw in some torture, decapitation, and lots of violence and you have a series you simply have to watch until the end.

Ultimate Survivor Put a group of strangers on an island, give them one item each and invite them to survive while trying to kill everybody else. It's like an insane version of Big Brother. Each episode has lots of laughs, blood and violence. It's definitely for those with a slightly sicker sense of humour than normal. Download and enjoy.

The Best of KillFrog Some excellent cartoons of questionable taste. These self-contained mini-stories are very professionally made with high-quality, vaguely adolescent humour. Fluff the Kitty and the Bunny Game are two great interactive cartoons which will appeal to those with a cruel streak. These are the best, but honestly, everything is worth a look.

Animations This is more of the same style humour, but everything here is a one off rather than part of a series. And here you can see something very odd, for Kill Frog – a cartoon with no violence. Have a look at One Last Dance, which is a dedication to Charles Schultz, the creator of Snoopy.

The Kat Play nasty interactive games or watch the cartoons, all at the expense of poor Kat's health.

Comics Some single cell cartoons, some satirical, some daft.

Downloads Now that you've seen then, you might want to download them to watch at your leisure.

Studio Ask those questions you just have to ask, like 'Why?'

A great site, well made, very funny, that some people will, unfortunately, hate.

comedy

| overall rating: |
| ★ ★ ★ ★ ★ |

| classification: |
| homepage |

| updated: |
| infrequently |

| navigation: |
| ★ ★ ★ ★ ★ |

| content: |
| ★ ★ ★ ★ ★ |

| readability: |
| ★ ★ ★ ★ ★ |

| speed: |
| ★ ★ ★ ★ |

| UK   18 |

http://www.superkaylo.com/super/html/main_menu.htm
Superkaylo

A cartoonist with too much time on his hands is a dangerous thing. This guy is busy writing for magazines and appearing on Radio One, but he still finds time to churn out cartoons that will offend virtually everyone. The probability is that if you like any one of these cartoons, you'll like them all. If you hate the first one, you'd better go elsewhere for your comedy. It's an interesting-looking site befitting an adult cartoon creator but, unfortunately, it isn't updated very often. Still, there's lots here already to make you laugh.

SPECIAL FEATURES

Muttworld Click on the arrows to scroll through a couple of very tasteless cartoons filled with doggie violence and sex.

Horny Estelle Unrequited lust is a terrible thing. Follow Estelle through some full-length adult comic strips, which first appeared in a comic called Elephant Parts.

Ring Pieces Crank calls of dubious sound quality.

Misc. Shit One offs, but the humour is still naked, violent and crude. And did we mention, funny?

Unnovations New innovations to make the world a better place, like the alarm clock that gives you 10 seconds to get out of bed before it stabs you in the head with a kitchen knife. Happy days.

Software Fictional products that stand no chance of ever making it into the shops. Then again, maybe there is a market for Nicholas Lyndhurst's Murder Party, where the well known comedy actor chases you round with an axe!

A brilliantly original and funny mind, who with a little more elbow grease could possibly achieve comedy world domination. Very funny site.

comedy

overall rating:	★ ★ ★ ★ ★
classification:	fan site
updated:	frequently
navigation:	★ ★ ★ ★
content:	★ ★ ★ ★ ★
readability:	★ ★ ★ ★
speed:	★ ★ ★ ★ ★
US	

www.snpp.com/lists.html
The Simpsons Archive

This site is not pretty by today's internet standards but that is not what its fanatical creators had in mind. What you get here is an enormous library of documents compiled by fans of the show. This must be one of the most amazingly detailed comedy sites out there. It's a trivia/list/fan paradise. To the occasional Simpsons viewer it's a hugely daunting site, but the confirmed fan of the show will think they've died and gone to Springfield.

SPECIAL FEATURES

Frequently Asked Questions This is much, much more than your usual FAQ. For starters, parts of it are available in up to seven different languages. A click on the List Of Inquiries And Substantive Answers then a scroll down to section three and The Episode Quicklist opens up a ridiculous and almost frightening amount of information. Click on any episode and you get quotes, jokes you might have missed, observations and lists and more worryingly detailed stuff.

Merchandise Information As well as details of all the books, recordings, trading cards and videos, there is also a list of mistakes from the official Simpsons book, information on where to find the Simpsons chess set and details on how to cheat your way to victory in a number of Simpsons games.

References Read the list of hundreds of magazine articles that just mentioned the show. Be amazed that there is a 36,000 word list of movie references in the show and other lists for Beatles, Music, dead people and references to death.

Springfield Info Okay, so you know about the people. But what about the place? This is where your need for house plans, newspaper headlines and golf course layout can be satisfied.

Fanfare This is less about the actual show and more to do with fans who have too much time on their hands. There's a trivia quiz, anagrams, and a test to see how 'pure' your worship of the show is.

Broadcast and Episode Info Everything you could possibly want to know about the show, its writers, directors, guest stars, the running gags and even the colours that are used when drawing the characters.

Automailers If you want information but don't have the time just now to read it all. Have a selection of the lists emailed to you.

Character Files These speak for themselves. However, as I'm sure you've guessed by now, the detail is amazing and content is huge.

Other Lists If you've got this far, these lists might be of interest. But if you're nothing more than a casual watcher, this will be out of your league, there are reference lists about theft, licence plates and even Mr T!

A site of encyclopaedic proportions. Not for everyone, but if it's facts and figures you're after, you'll never leave the house again.

comedy

overall rating: ★ ★ ★ ★	
classification: official site	
updated: fortnightly	
navigation: ★ ★ ★ ★	
content: ★ ★ ★ ★ ★	
readability: ★ ★ ★ ★ ★	
speed: ★ ★ ★	
UK	

http://www.henson.com
Henson.com

One of the enormous pluses of this site is that it caters for all types of fans of Henson shows. The icons across the top take you to some fascinating information on both the business and professional sides of the Henson company, while the green section running up and down the middle of the page is aimed at a younger audience with masses of fun and games featuring the characters themselves. It's wonderful to look at, but some of the graphics, especially in Muppet World, take a long time to load. It's worth mentioning that Henson.com is simply an umbrella site for the links in the green area. Many of these links take you to sites in their own rights, with every link opening up a number of new ones.

SPECIAL FEATURES

Creators At the top of the page, the icon of Jim Henson takes you to what must be one of the most important and yet least known areas of the company. Here you can find detailed information about the humans involved in shows like the Muppets. Friends and colleagues remember Jim and a detailed biography fills in some gaps. There are also details of the puppeteers. And once you've learnt all about them, find out how they do what they do with the Muppet Workshop.

The Puppet Café Watch puppetry from around the world, so long as you've got a fast computer and the necessary plug-ins.

Muppet World   An enormous site of interactive fun and games and info on Kermit and his fellow Muppets, aimed predominantly at children. Again, this is a wonderfully visual dedication to the programme, so be prepared to give up your evening waiting for things to load. Many of the features, however, are worth the long wait.

Sesame Workshop   Entertaining and educational fun for children, with a very American section for parents, including things to read to your child when they've got the 'grouchies'.

OTHER FEATURES

There is also a dedicated section on the Mopatops, Bear in the Big Blue House and a section on Odyssey, the Henson-owned TV Channel where you can watch lots of the shows.

A well-designed, great looking site with loads of content for young and old. Fun and informative, it's a must for all fans of Henson and the Muppets.

comedy

overall rating: ★ ★ ★ ★	
classification: fan site	
updated: frequently	
navigation: ★ ★ ★	
content: ★ ★ ★ ★	
readability: ★ ★ ★	
speed: ★ ★ ★	
AUS	

http://www.bugsbunnyburrow.com
The Bugs Bunny Burrow

At first glance, this huge Loony Tunes site is a little clumsy. The front page is like a scrapbook of sponsor ads and links and, apart from some downloads, there is no mention of what you can find inside – or even how to get in. But once you find and click on the drop down box at the top of the page which says Bounce the Burrow, you'll see that this site has a lot more to offer than simply commercial sponsors, even if the navigation still takes a little getting used to. Your initial click takes you to your page of choice, but then a second drop-down box appears where the first was and the first box moves to the centre of the new page. Once you're into the site the boxes stay where they are and suddenly it all makes sense. You'll soon get the hang of it. The site hasn't been around for long but it is already huge and updated fairly frequently.

SPECIAL FEATURES

The Burrow Store Although the site doesn't actually sell you anything itself, there are loads of things to buy. Simply click on one of over 60 links under Select Department and you will be taken to an appropriate online store to buy the item. There's lots on offer and secure online purchasing means you can buy with greater confidence.

Games/Themes/Skins, etc. All manner of downloads, including animated cursors, fonts, start-up and shutdown screens. If you like your computer to reflect your comedy tastes, you'll be pleased to see that there are several dozen complete desktop themes for you to install.

Behind the Scenes Everything you could possibly want to know about your favourite Loony Tunes characters and the talent that created them and gave them voices. Then, when you've spent the best part of the day reading all that, there are the forgotten cartoons, the voices you've never heard of and even a list of the characters' birthdays.

Get Interactive! All the stuff that wouldn't fit anywhere else, a lot of which is less interesting than the rest of the site. However, you can send in your own Loony Tune drawings and have them posted on the site, read cheats for Loony Tunes games, get more cartoon links, sign up for emailed updates and get your own Loony Tunes email address.

OTHER FEATURES

You can also find pages of screensavers, pictures, great classic sounds and more wallpaper than B&Q.

A busy site that works hard to provide for all your Loony Tune needs.

comedy

overall rating: ★★★★	
classification: fan site	
updated: occasionally	
navigation: ★★★★★	
content: ★★★★	
readability: ★★★★	
speed: ★★★★★	
US	

http://members.optushome.com.au/webrock
The Flintstones and Hanna-Barbera

Everyone remembers The Flintstones, and a wander round this informative site will bring more memories flooding back. It's a dedicated fan site, so if you're not a fan there's nothing to interest you. The design is simple by today's standards, but the navigation couldn't be easier. All the links to other sections are right there on the front page. Started in 1995 by a Flintstones fan, it claims to be the longest-running Flintstones site on the internet. It has just about everything you could want to know about the show, and other Hanna-Barbera cartoons. The only downside is the fact that the site is low tech, and has no interactive element or particularly interesting graphics. And the music that plays on the front page. It never stops. Ever.

SPECIAL FEATURES

HB Links Strange that the first button is a links button, offering to take you elsewhere. However, with over 80 links to a variety of cartoon sites, this is worth a look if you're after something specific and not in the mood for simply browsing.

HB Shows From Abbott and Costello to Yogi's Treasure Hunt, if Hanna-Barbera produced it, it's probably here. Dozens of shows you watched as a child and thought you had forgotten. Many of the cartoons have links to personal sites of their own.

HB Sounds Downloadable sound files from some cartoons and a selection of lyrics so you can sing along to your old favourites.

HB Trivia Rather than telling you trivia, this page asks you questions. If you don't know or prefer cheating, which is highly likely, the answers are there in the drop-down box at the end of the question.

Bedrock City The Flintstones now have their very own theme park in South Dakota. This is a brief review of a visit there.

Fun & Games Send an e-card, get stuff for your desktop, puzzles, games, and even pictures to colour in. However, be warned, the games are not interactive but are simply pictures to print and then 'play', a maze, a word game and a dot-to-dot. If you want more there are a few links to other games on the net.

Flintstones FAQ Did you know The Flintstones was originally called The Flagstones? There are lots of other interesting questions and lots of expert answers.

Flintstones Trivia Again, many of the facts test your Flintstones knowledge and ask questions rather than just listing interesting titbits. If you're not a fan you've got no chance.

Flintstones Movie Links to reviews of the first Flintstones film and some original photos. It's a shame that the site owner didn't do a review herself, as most of these film links lead to short, disappointing information.

Flintstones Episodes Titles, writers, recording dates, air dates and a synopsis of the original series, which ran for six years.

Buy, Sell or Trade Be amazed at how many Flintstones fans want to buy and sell memorabilia. Easy to use, it puts buyers and

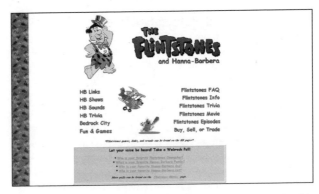

sellers in touch with each other but accepts no responsibility for what happens after you part with your cash.

The Flintstones and Hanna-Barbera Bulletin Board The link is further down the opening page. Mostly it's fans advertising their own sites, asking cartoon-related questions and trying to buy stuff. However, if you've got something to say it's easy to use.

Brilliant for Flintstones information and a good place to start for other Hanna-Barbera cartoons.

http://www.aardman.com/wallaceandgromit/index.shtml
West Wallaby on the Web

The official home of Wallace and Gromit. It's run by Aardman, the company who made the films, so you can be sure it's accurate. It's easy to navigate, with the four main links in the middle of the front page. It's simply but very attractively designed, too. You'll find everything you expect from a normal fan site, like sound bites and pictures, but there is also detailed information about the making of the films which you are unlikely to find elsewhere. Unfortunately, it's rarely updated these days.

SPECIAL FEATURES

Cheese and Crackers Most interesting are the sound bites. They are just the right size to add to your system sounds. There are also some slightly pointless animated gifs and an animated rocket that spins faster or slower depending on how far your mouse is from it.

Film Pages Each of the films has a link to its own page, including fascinating notes on the production and pictures from the film. The Wrong Trousers has an original storyboard slideshow. It's the sort of information no fan site can have.

62 West Wallaby Street Click on the character icons to be taken to their own page. There are also some more pictures that you can download.

overall rating:
★ ★ ★ ★

classification:
official site

updated:
rarely

navigation:
★ ★ ★ ★ ★

content:
★ ★ ★ ★

readability:
★ ★ ★ ★

speed:
★ ★ ★ ★

UK

Wallace's Workshop The claim 'Where anything might happen!' is a little misleading. What actually happens is another storyboard slideshow, an odd feature where you can change Wallace's appearance at the click of a button, and a jigsaw puzzle to complete online.

OTHER FEATURES

You can also send a Wallace and Gromit postcard and order memorabilia from Amazon.

Colourful and fun, with some real insider information you won't find anywhere else.

http://www.magicpen.net
Magicpen

A lot of animation on the internet is created by expert animators for no good reason other than to amuse themselves and show off their talents. This is one such website and a good place to start to experience web animation. Although the humour on this relatively small site floats around the level of 'greetings card' puns, Gary Davison's artwork itself is excellent. The layout is simple but impressive, and a variety of sounds add to your viewing pleasure. Unfortunately, as with all sites like this, there is a fairly long wait while each cartoon loads, and if you haven't got Flash technology installed the animations won't appear. The content is updated sporadically.

SPECIAL FEATURES

Animation This is the backbone of the site, where the true talent lies. At present there are only six animated cartoons, but more are promised. All take a while to load, but being animation, you have to expect that.

Cartoons Again, the humour is more card shop than comedy store, and with only four cartoons the section would benefit from some expansion.

Interactive Sounds interesting. Probably will be. For the moment, it's nothing more than an annoying notice claiming the page will be 'Coming Soon'.

overall rating:	★ ★ ★
classification:	homepage
updated:	occasionally
navigation:	★ ★ ★ ★ ★
content:	★ ★ ★
readability:	★ ★ ★ ★
speed:	★ ★ ★
US	

Contact This is where the guestbook is hidden for you to post messages. So far nothing but nice things have been said about the site and its creator. Alternatively you could send an email to Gary himself, he doesn't seem to mind.

Links Split into sections, your two choices are Soul Food (entertaining sites) and Brain Food (helpful sites). Not much choice, but as it's Gary's site he can do what he likes.

When you accidentally point your mouse over the site logo, up pops a hidden title: News. This is little more than a greeting and a promise of more to come. That really sums up the site. It's clever, smooth, and there's plenty of talent there, but it needs more content.

OTHER SITES OF INTEREST
http://www.scuffmark.com
Scuffmark.com
18

If you liked Joe Cartoon and Kill Frog, and you have a fast computer and modem to cope with the long download times, you'll love this too. More blood and gore are on offer here, and all in the spirit of alternative cartoon humour. There are some particularly interesting interactive games, too, two of the best being 'Duelling Gentlemen' and 'Dr Dentist'. If you don't like violence or cruelty to cartoon animals, stay away.

the written word

Behind every funny cartoon, gag, sketch, humorous book, comedy show or film, there's a writer. Alone, but for his scribblings, and an ever growing mountain of coffee cups, he struggles to bring a smile to your face. If he's lucky, he does it for money; if not, he does it because he has to, driven by some inner urge to have no friends or social life, save for the relationship between himself and that blank sheet of paper.

But, hey, who said life was going to be easy? All these sites are dedicated to people who write or draw their humour. A few of them even invite you to have a go yourself. And why not? We've all watched something and thought: 'I could do better than that.' Can you? Are you sure?

The range of comedy here is enormous, from well-known characters familiar with children to the outpourings of semi-deranged comedy types, obsessed with bodily functions and political incorrectness. The kind of people who sit next to you on an otherwise empty train. They're all here. Enjoy.

http://www.garfield.com
Garfield on-line

Garfield might spend most of his time bored or asleep, but at this official Garfield site you'll be amazed at how much is going on. The homepage looks a little jumbled at first glance, but once you start clicking down the yellow buttons down the left-hand side everything is far more organised. One of the great design features is the constant use of clickable links within the text. Some of these take you to other relevant places of interest, while others produce great pop-up cartoons. The site has a fun and sometimes downright daft tone to it, and is worth every second you spend browsing.

SPECIAL FEATURES

What's Hot This page has links to the hottest Garfield happenings around the internet. Recently, there were a couple of downloads, details of a collectors' contest and news of a recent award.

Comics Most of us know the fat ginger cat from those three cell cartoons in the papers. Using the links further down the page, you can read masses of published comic-strips. You can also get character profiles and Fat Cat Facts. (Did you know that Garfield's best friend is his mirror?) For the real low-down, backed up with comic-strip evidence, have a look at The Wide World Of Garfield.

Many of the strips can be bought online, by post or over the
phone. They are obviously bigger than you would find in a
newspaper, and for more money can be bought already framed.
Once you've added shipping charges, though, they do work out
quite expensive. If you want something for free, why not
download a short Video Clip featuring Garfield and his chums,
or print up a black and white picture of the cat himself and
colour it in?

Fun and Games There are loads of games and fun things to
download. They all take a little while so you have to be patient.
The graphics are great and the games are actually interesting
enough to make you play them more than once. There are also
the usual backgrounds, wallpaper and some icons to add to
your desktop. Also good fun is the online colouring and the e-
cards you can send to friends. There's a chat room too, but it's
closed at the moment.

Garfield Gazette Get up-to-the-minute news and stuff from
around the world. There's also some very informative stuff about
what goes on behind the scenes in the world of Garfield, with
information about Jim Davis, the author, and the company
behind the fat orange cat.

OTHER FEATURES

Book Nook Get all your Garfield books sent to your door,
although you would be better off looking for the titles in a British
online book store; these links will have your order posted from
America.

Online Catalog Garfield products available to buy the world over, like those cute little fellas suckered to the inside of car windows. The Garfield Guarantee explains in simple, no fuss language their

terms and conditions, and online security.

Fan Club If you love Garfield that much, why not join his fan club? Be warned though, it's not free.

Bob's Legal Stuff If you're thinking about downloading from this site, then this section is worth a quick glance. There's lots of humour amongst the legal stuff which makes it quite a fun read.

An excellent site all round. The brilliant Garfield comic strips alone make it worth the visit.

comedy

overall rating:	★ ★ ★ ★ ★
classification:	official site
updated:	frequently
navigation:	★ ★ ★ ★ ★
content:	★ ★ ★ ★ ★
readability:	★ ★ ★ ★ ★
speed:	★ ★ ★ ★
US	

http://www.snoopy.com
Snoopy.com

Being read in 2,600 newspapers, by 350 million people a day is pretty good evidence that Peanuts is indeed the most popular comic strip in history. If the site is anything to go by, it will continue to be for some time. Right from the familiar daily cartoon you know you're in for a good time here. There's recent Peanuts news under the cartoon. Further down there are links for Kids, Grown-Ups and Collectors.

But if you have no idea who you are or how you fit into the world of Snoopy, start with the links in the yellow box on the left. It's a quick site, fairly attractive to look at, and will appeal to all the family. It's also updated frequently, so well worth a regular visit.

SPECIAL FEATURES
Strip Library If you do nothing else you'll want to look at some cartoons. The drop down box has one a day for the last month.

History There is a clickable Timeline which takes you to occasions throughout the history of Snoopy and his friends. However, Around The Globe may have been a mistake. Cartoons that are exactly the same as the originals but with the words in a different language is not a terribly exciting idea. The Play Peanuts Trivia link is a good idea, but we had problems connecting to it.

Profiles A brief background to each of the characters in the comic strip and a couple of cartoons featuring each one. including their very first appearance in print.

Fun and games Postcards, word puzzles, a surprisingly difficult interactive baseball game, pictures to colour in, online or off. Short movies to watch and cursors you can download to your PC.

The Store A collectors heaven. Official merchandise galore. Lists and lists of Peanuts stuff to spend your money on, so long as you live in the USA. They won't ship to Britain, but at least you know what's available and can try searching for it elsewhere on the web.

Charles Schultz Read a biography of the great man who invented and drew all the cartoon strips, and read details of the Schultz museum. You can also click on links to 100 tributes to Charles Schultz drawn by other cartoonists. Sadly, only a handful of the cartoons are popular in Britain. The Garfield one is particularly touching.

OTHER FEATURES

The Clubhouse There are details of where you can see and hear the Peanuts gang in America. This includes, for those who care, which shopping items will be displaying the characters on their packaging.

There will be no more original cartoons but this site has everything to keep the Peanuts memory alive.

comedy

overall rating: ★ ★ ★ ★ ★	
classification: guide	
updated: occasionally	
navigation: ★ ★ ★ ★ ★	
content: ★ ★ ★ ★	
readability: ★ ★ ★ ★ ★	
speed: ★ ★ ★	
UK	

http://www.comedyzone.beeb.com/comedy/bestof/features/writestuff/script_welcome.html
The Write Stuff

The 'Official site of the BBC's Comedy Script Unit'. It's a text-based guide that wastes no time trying to impress you with crazy graphics or pointless features. Ignore the links down the left of the page, they refer to the parent site, the BBC's Comedy Zone, information about which is listed elsewhere in this guide. Down the right-hand side are links to shopping. All you need to interest yourself with are the five icons at the top of the page, which take you to a minefield of information. Don't forget, the BBC are in the habit of making the odd television programme, so they know what they're talking about. And when you've finished your first script, using their guidelines, why not send it to them first and see what they think? The site can be a little sluggish at times, but it's worth the wait.

SPECIAL FEATURES
Writer's Guidelines You may not have the experience, you may not have the raw talent, you may not even have a sense of humour; but, once you've digested these comprehensive guidelines, you'll certainly know how to start, and how to avoid many of the common pitfalls that get scripts rejected. You'll also know how to submit your script and what will happen to

it when it arrives at the BBC. You'll almost certainly be miles ahead of other writers who have not studied these guidelines. There is a separate but equally thorough section for Light Entertainment Radio, which also includes information on writing sketch shows and panel games.

Then there are also addresses to send your finished work to, and extremely useful templates which you can load into your word processor so that your formatting is exactly right. Unfortunately, the templates will only work on Word 7.

Resources The most frequently asked questions get answered here. There's some recommended reading if you want more background on the writing task facing you. Finally, there are links to some useful websites for the budding writer to visit.

Workshop Coming soon, a free course on comedy script writing. Not much news at the moment, but definitely something to keep an eye on.

The Writer's Room You can read your informative copy of the monthly newsletter here. There are interesting articles to make sure your script has the best possible chance for success. If you're still stuck, you could pop into the Forum and discuss your problems with other writers; if the page is up and working, that is. At the time of review, it seems to have disappeared.

This might not be a funny site, but if you have an interest in creating comedy, especially situation comedy, it's absolutely invaluable.

comedy

overall rating:	★ ★ ★ ★ ★
classification:	adult comic
updated:	monthly
navigation:	★ ★ ★ ★ ★
content:	★ ★ ★ ★
readability:	★ ★ ★ ★ ★
speed:	★ ★ ★ ★
UK 18	

http://www.viz.co.uk
VIZ

Not for children. At all.

The adult comic that has become a cult read for all students, band members and people who want a laugh in an 'I know it's adolescent, but I don't care' kind of way, can be equally proud of its well-designed site. It's full colour with lots of pictures and yet still loads pretty quickly. If you've never seen a copy of the comic you may be taken aback by the wealth of bad language, sex and politically incorrect material that bombards you from the very first page. If you have seen a copy before, you'll know what you're doing and will easily slip into the required state of silliness and comic euphoria. The site links run colourfully down the left-hand side of the page.

SPECIAL FEATURES
Latest Issue Not surprisingly, this is a review/advert for the current paper issue available in the shops. A few of the comic strips can be viewed online.

Free Downloads Leave your maturity at the door and download silly games that you wouldn't want your mother to see.

Subscribe to this Filth Not a link to get updates for the site, but details of how to have childish filth shoved through your letterbox every two months, or 'a subscription to Viz' as it's sometimes known.

Hairloom Collectibles Rubbish and nasty tat for you to buy. And at only £20 each, that's surely next Christmas sorted out.

The Crypt of Crap Dreadful cartoons. Er, that's it.

Roger's Profanisaurus A brilliantly infantile idea. Take every rude word or phrase you've ever heard of, or just made up for the hell of it and explain it dictionary style. Hilarious reading. You're encouraged to send in suggestions of your own. Extremely offensive.

Viz is the opposite end of the spectrum from honest to goodness, wholesome fun and japes for all the family, but it simply cannot be ignored because, quite simply, it's funny.

comedy

overall rating: ★ ★ ★ ★	
classification: homepage	
updated: monthly	
navigation: ★ ★ ★ ★	
content: ★ ★ ★ ★	
readability: ★ ★ ★ ★	
speed: ★ ★ ★ ★ ★	
US	

http://home.earthlink.net/~cgerena/duh.htm
Duh

Very simply, the world's a crazy place and no mistake. What we have here is a small but perfectly formed collection of actual news stories that make you wonder what hope there is for us as the reigning species on the planet. There is nothing complex in the site design, but it does have some cheerful animated icons which take you straight to the most recent individual news stories with a single click. Once there, you'll find a vaguely related and completely pointless sound to download and listen to while you read.

SPECIAL FEATURES

Want More? Not really a feature, just a link to more stories. Don't worry about being swamped with hundreds of links; as with the rest of this site, they've aimed for quality over quantity. Which is a bit of a shame, as sometimes the quality is a bit poor.

A Warning to Stupid People Funny. Well worth downloading and sending to your friends. Everyone knows someone who should take heed of this advice.

Feedback If you've ever had a run-in with stupidity, here's the place to share it with the world. Or maybe you would rather just share a thought – any thought – with the readers? That's allowed too. Just click on Your 2 Cents at the bottom of any page and follow the instructions.

DUH Library A few links to some books on a similar theme, including The Book of Duh. All the links take you to Amazon, where you can search more specifically if these titles are not to your liking.

It's a Gusher...For Stupid Politicians Don't you love it when the people in charge prove themselves to be really stupid? Some political idiocy to poke fun at. However, it's all American and there's not enough to choose from.

It's not ground breaking or flashy, but a lot of the content is funny, if only in a 'what a prat!' kind of way. Best of all, it's true.

comedy

overall rating: ★★★★	
classification: homepage	
updated: weekly	
navigation: ★★★★★	
content: ★★★★	
readability: ★★★★	
speed: ★★★	
UK	

http://www.planetcomedy.co.uk/home.html
Planet Comedy

Planet Comedy write scripts for television and radio. The sort of thing your parents don't understand, it's modern, sassy and probably works better with added alcohol. Their uncomplicated site is not terribly attractive to look at, but it contains a variety of comedy-related items and is updated weekly. Down the left of the page are links to things they think are funny and down the centre of the page are the things Planet Comedy are up to professionally. The right-hand side is reserved for news of their varied successes. There is some genuinely funny and original stuff here, but the single most interesting parts of the site are those that cover the art of writing comedy. If you've ever wanted to write and sell your own comedy, or ever wondered how they think of this stuff, there is some very useful advice here.

SPECIAL FEATURES

Funny Stuff Funny Poems is a dedication to Brian Luff, a comedy poet amusingly described as 'wickedly poor', but really quite outrageously funny. He's rude, obnoxious, and if you don't find him even a little bit funny, you've missed the point.

Sketches contains actual scripts for sketches that were shown on TV, which is a good way of seeing how the professionals do it. Even without the aid of TV, they're pretty funny.

Newsflash is an annoying link to a sponsor's search engine.

Liar Media is a link to another site with news stories and information that is simply not true.

Essential TV Smack the Pony, Father Ted, Eric Morecambe and Big Train may well be essential comedy viewing, but these links all take you to sub-standard pages which are hardly worth bothering with. The Big Train page even admits to being 'hastily cobbled together'. It shows.

Resources Planet Comedy give their views on books for comedy writers and funny books in general. There isn't much to choose from but these guys write comedy for a living so their opinions just might be trustworthy. There are also some links to various comedy sites.

Extras Apart from some very funny one-liners taken from the Montreal Comedy festival, there is little here worth visiting.

Comedy Writing Guide This is what you really want, and it makes visiting the site worthwhile. However, clicking this link doesn't immediately take you to the guide. Instead, it takes you to a page where you can sign up for 'Pants On Fire', Planet Comedy's e-zine. When your first copy arrives, scroll down to the bottom and you'll find an active link to the article you want. Not very convenient, but if you want to write sketch comedy and are just starting out, it's priceless.

Attractive it isn't, but they're writers rather than designers; and if you're a budding comedy writer looking for help, that's all that matters.

comedy

overall rating: ★ ★ ★ ★	
classification: fan guide	
updated: monthly	
navigation: ★ ★ ★ ★	
content: ★ ★ ★ ★	
readability: ★ ★ ★	
speed: ★ ★ ★ ★ ★	
UK	

http://www.co.uk.lspace.org
The L-Space Web (Terry Pratchett/Discworld)

The site has been around since 1994, and these guys know their stuff. Terry Pratchett is one of the world's most popular authors but he is still seen as a writer for students, geeks and fantasy freaks. However, his books are clever, funny and quite unlike anything else around. If you're a fan you can learn more about Pratchett and the Discworld series. If you're new to Pratchett, this website might get you hooked. The main links run up and down the front page and are like chapter headings, in that they take you to information and further links rather than to a single page. It's not attractive by current standards, but these guys deal in information rather than aesthetics. Be warned, though; this site is populated by experts. You might feel as if you've wandered into a smoky library full of stuffy Professors who all turn to stare at you the minute you walk through the door.

SPECIAL FEATURES

Terry Pratchett The biography's main concern is Pratchett's writing history, but if you want something else try the alt.fan.pratchett FAQ link to a slightly confusing list of lists of places where Pratchett fans swap information. Terry often joins in discussions on Pratchett newsgroups, and some of his more memorable comments have been collected in the Pratchett Quote File: 'This isn't life in the fast lane, it's life in the oncoming traffic.' You can also get photos, and interviews.

Books and Writings This is another of those sections where dangerous obsessives masquerading as fans churn out facts and figures about things you never thought about. If you like lists and trivia you'll love it. If not, you may need to lie down in a dark room for a couple of hours.

The Annotated Pratchett File reads like the world's most detailed A-level pass notes. Individual lines are examined for relevance. This is way more detail than most human beings can cope with without exploding.

You can get a taste for the comedy in the Pratchett Quote File. Every book is listed with some choice quotes.

The Discworld Who's Who Surprisingly, this section is no longer being updated. It would surely have been one of the most useful places for a new fan to visit; more useful, you might think, than the Deaths List, which pointlessly lists all the people who die in each of the books.

OTHER FEATURES

Art and Graphics, FAQs, details of where like-minded Pratchett fans get together (both on the net and in the flesh) in Fan Activity, Merchandise and, at the time of review, 98 links in Other Resources.

The site is not as enjoyable as the books, but after a bit of a browse you'll find yourself getting sucked into a completely new world with more detail than the real one.

comedy

overall rating: ★ ★ ★ ★	
classification: newspaper	
updated: weekly	
navigation: ★ ★ ★ ★	
content: ★ ★ ★ ★	
readability: ★ ★ ★ ★	
speed: ★ ★ ★ ★	
US 18	

http://www.theonion.com
The Onion

With newspapers and news programmes reporting so much doom and gloom, The Onion could be the perfect weekly to lift your spirits. Why Onion? Because there's layer after layer of quality humour? Because it will have tears rolling down your cheeks? Not quite. It does have its moments, though; for example, there's a thoughtful article on the development of the first e-toilet and also a harrowing report of a student and an enormous cockroach. Bear in mind these are fictional stories, written with the creative tongue firmly in the creative cheek. There is some clever satire and some absolute nonsense, but it's written in a tight, journalistic style that makes some of the news nearly believable.

The simple design makes the stories easy to read, and graphics are kept small so there's not much waiting for pages to appear. The main page shows this week's edition, while links on the left of the page take you to older news stories. The only downside is that all the story content is American; occasionally, the reports have little or no relevance to a non-American reader.

SPECIAL FEATURES
News Archives You can search for stories by subject here. The link takes you to opening paragraphs of stories, so you can make an even more informed choice on what to read.

Editorial Archives Each link takes you to a particular weekly columnist. Particularly good are T. Herman Zweibel, a cantankerous and bedridden old moaner, and Jackie Harvey, a hopelessly ill-informed and scatty celebrity commentator. The style for each columnist is pretty repetitive, so if you read a couple and they don't make you laugh, move on to someone else. Also very funny are the Ask a... where characters like 'A Chat Room' and 'A Gut-Shot Policeman' answer readers' questions. Some people will find this section tasteless.

Clever, satirical, American. But forget it if you're looking for ordinary gags and jokes.

comedy

overall rating:	★ ★ ★
classification:	newspaper
updated:	not
navigation:	★ ★ ★ ★ ★
content:	★ ★ ★
readability:	★ ★ ★
speed:	★ ★ ★ ★
CAN	

http://members.aol.com/thewebloid
The Very Silly Webloid

People who always say how 'mad and crazy' they are often turn out to be quite uninteresting. In the same way, any site that feels the need to tell you that it is 'very silly' immediately gets you thinking that it isn't. Which is about half right for this site. Each issue has three or four stories which are often backed up by amusing fake photos. Bill Clinton 'admitted' to the assassination of Kennedy in a recent issue, and the confession was backed up by a previously unseen photo of Clinton with Lee Harvey Oswald. That's about the standard. Many of the stories are a single idea stretched to the required word length. If you like the original idea, then great. If not, not. The site looks quite good and is quick to download. The most recent issue is towards the bottom of the homepage and links to older copies are near the top on the right. For the foreseeable future, what you see is what you get as no more issues are planned.

SPECIAL FEATURES
The First Ten Back Issues Quite hit and miss. There are some excellent stories, including one about a choreographer who specialises in the top half of the body being incensed that all his work has been cut from Riverdance, and then there are features like the Classified Ads, which raise only the occasional smile.

Some Of Our Reviews: Are We Chuffed! This is not really a feature, but does include one of the funniest things on the site.

For the Jerusalem Post to state 'Now Canada has a humour magazine on the web', and for this site to herald it as a review to be chuffed about should make you fall off your chair.

This is a really good idea but the humour tends more towards smiles than belly-laughs.

OTHER SITES OF INTEREST

Disturbed Poetry Corner

http://www.comedyzine.com/poemindex.shtml

18

Most people don't like poetry. But don't be put off, this site isn't aimed at people who 'like' it. If you think poetry has nothing to do with your life and should be left to drippy romantics and depressed students then you might well enjoy this site. You won't get 'I wandered lonely as a cloud' but 'I Met My True Love At The Clinic', 'Graveyard Zombie' and 'Popping Pimples'. Lots of stuff to offend everyone you ever met as well as some very disturbing words from some extremely dodgy people.

Private Eye

http://www.private-eye.co.uk/frames/index.htm

Private Eye is like Earl Grey, you have to have a taste for it. Which would probably explain why it's not everybody's cup of tea. To some it's the height of satire. It's cutting and quick and witty. To the rest of us, however, the problem is that it conjures up images of Oxbridge students in big scarves, standing together in corners giggling cleverly. This, frankly, is reason enough to immediately look elsewhere. However, if you still like to potter around in your old school tie you'll be glad to know the site is simplistic and easy to navigate. There are some features from the paper and you're encouraged to subscribe. You can also buy back issues and place small ads for insertion in the printed version. Scarf collectors' clubs and that kind of thing.

The Far Side Fan Page
http://www.someone.force9.co.uk/far_side.html

You've seen Gary Larson's cards, books, calendars, T-shirts and dozens of other items covered with his Far Side cartoons. They're some of the funniest cartoons ever. But if you've ever looked for The Far Side on the internet you'll have found most of the sites closed down, displaying letters from Gary explaining how his cartoons are his children and how he doesn't like to find his work on the net without his knowledge. And he throws his weight about by mentioning 'lawyers'. Oh dear, oh dear. But here's a site still at large. Enjoy the brilliant Far Side online while you still can.

WhiteBoard News
http://www.joeha.com/whiteboard

It couldn't be more boring to look at if it tried. However, if you're after more up-to-the-minute true-life stories from around the world, this will be right up your street. With up to 14 issues a month, each containing five or six stories, there's plenty to remind you that if you made it up people wouldn't believe you. The humour is hit and miss, but it's more fun to read than your local free paper.

tv

From the comfort of your own chair, you will have sat in front of the television and passed judgement on dozens of programmes claiming to be 'comedies'. Quite frankly, some of them have been downright dreadful and some of them still are. However, from the comfort of your chair in front of the computer you can now access any number of sites dedicated to the very best TV comedy as, generally, it's only the good shows that have sites made about them.

Of course, that's not to say that the site is going to be any good just because it's a good programme. Oh, the trials and tribulations of the internet. There are absolutely hundreds of TV comedy web sites that are not covered in the next few pages, but of the best shows, these are the best sites. If you don't agree? Well, we'll see you in court.

http://www.blackadderhall.co.uk
Blackadder Hall

A great feeling of history wafts up from the monitor as you begin to wander around the rooms of this great ancestral home. However, surprisingly for a site dedicated to a series that finished quite some time ago, it is still lovingly updated on a fairly regular basis, and has recently undergone a complete face lift. There is no multimedia here, but if you want information and detail you've come to the right place. To find your way around, click on the links on the left of the opening page. The latest site updates are on the main page too, just click on the pointy fingers next to the snippets.

SPECIAL FEATURES

The Series A different link for each of the four series. You'll find brief episode plot descriptions, cast and production lists and, at the bottom of each section, a link to either a quiz or quotes, or both.

The Specials Superb details of all the Blackadder specials, sketches and even the pilot episode. There are script transcripts and background details, and Blackadder Back and Forth has some wonderful photos. It makes for excellent reading.

Blackadder Stuff This contains all the bits and pieces that wouldn't fit anywhere else. The best bits are below.

overall rating:	★ ★ ★ ★ ★
classification:	fan site
updated:	regularly
navigation:	★ ★ ★ ★ ★
content:	★ ★ ★ ★
readability:	★ ★ ★ ★
speed:	★ ★ ★ ★ ★
UK	

News Frequently updated news about releases of new material and murmurs from around the world about all things Blackadder.

The Blackadder Shop A comprehensive list of books, CDs, videos and recordings related to the Blackadder series.

Library Interviews, transcripts and official press releases This is also where you will find the Frequently Asked Questions, which are an interesting read.

Fun 'n' Games Five quizzes to see how much you remember, and how much of a fan you really are.

An Audience With... Got a problem? Need something sorting out? Tell King Edmund and see what he can do. This is a brand new feature, which at the time of writing has not had any posts.

OTHER FEATURES

There are also short sections on Gardening with Baldrick and cooking with Mrs. Miggins. Also, fill in your email address in the box on the top right of the page and have news, rumour and gossip sent directly to you by email.

Excellent as it is, filled with heaps of information, this site would be even better still if it had more pictures, sounds and multimedia content.

http://britcoms.com
Britcoms.com

overall rating: ★ ★ ★ ★ ★
classification: fan guide
updated: weekly
navigation: ★ ★ ★ ★
content: ★ ★ ★ ★ ★
readability: ★ ★ ★ ★
speed: ★ ★ ★ ★ ★
US

If you ever needed proof that the Americans love the British sense of humour, then look no further. Britcoms is a nice-looking site, with a few flaws. The clock proclaiming London Time isn't right. It's an hour fast. But you have your watch, wall clocks and even your computer to tell you the actual time, so you don't have to worry about that. This American fan has collected information about British comedies, supposedly for other Americans, but his site is useful to anyone looking for specific links, wherever you're from. You can get around the site by clicking the blue buttons on the left of the screen, then clicking the new button that appears.

SPECIAL FEATURES

Web Sites/Britcom Sites   From Absolutely Fabulous to The Young Ones, this alphabetical list takes you, in the opinion of the host, to a really good site dedicated to that comedy. On the whole the sites are very good, but the odd one has closed down or is no longer maintained. An excellent list of shows, new and old, from all sides of the comedy spectrum.

Videos/Britcom Videos   Opening with extremely dramatic music, this page hosts a huge collection of comedy videos. Click the alphabetical tabs at the top of the page for lists of situation comedies that have videos available to buy. Click on the title to be taken to the online retailer. However, remember that all these videos here are sold through the USA version of Amazon, priced in dollars and often in a format that will not play on a British video player. If you find something you want, search for it in the British arm of Amazon at Amazon.co.uk.

Links/Comedy Links A list of links to British performers, and other situation comedy sites that are good but didn't make it onto the main list. Hover your mouse over the word Info and a little background on the site pops up. Click Go to go there.

Newsletter/Britcom Times Have news of new releases sent straight to your Inbox. There are lots of ad links to whet your appetite and news of things comedic and British as and when appropriate.

If you want specifically British humour, Britcoms.com can point you in the direction of some excellent sites. Takes the hassle out of searching for what you want.

http://www.phill.co.uk
British TV Comedy Resources

An excellent British television comedy site of encyclopaedic proportions, with loads of cross-referenced information. It is informative, well designed and extremely user-friendly. Lots of different areas are inter-linked, so browsing is very easy. Right from the first page you're given lots of choices and information. There are lists of the most recent additions and changes, recommended reading and viewing, as well as links to some of the classics of television comedy. The main parts of the site are found by clicking the six links to the right of the title. These links are available from each part of the site, so there is no need to keep clicking the back button to find what you need. Any time you want to get back to the first page, simply click on the Resources button. There are just enough photos to keep the site interesting and enjoyable without making the pages take an age to load. And it's getting bigger, with updates almost every day.

overall rating:	★ ★ ★ ★ ★
classification:	fan guide
updated:	daily
navigation:	★ ★ ★ ★ ★
content:	★ ★ ★ ★ ★
readability:	★ ★ ★ ★ ★
speed:	★ ★ ★ ★ ★
UK	

SPECIAL FEATURES

Books An excellent list of scripts and tie-ins. Click on the title of the book and you'll be taken to a very short description with details of the writer, publisher and a link to purchase the book there and then online.

Programmes The new additions and the revised pages are listed here to keep you up to date with what's been happening at the site. At the top of the page, click on a letter and you'll get an index of comedy programmes beginning with that letter. There is an incredible number of programmes covered. At the bottom of the page is a list to the 60 most frequently searched programmes on the site. Clicking on any programme title, anywhere in the site, takes you to its own page, where you'll find cast and episode details, details of videos that may be available and links that may be of further interest to you. Very comprehensive.

Videos Lots of excellent titles that you can buy online. Clicking the Video Sources link gives you details of places to look if you're after something specific. You'll also find news of the most recent comedy releases.

People All the most famous names from British television comedy. Click on their name for a list of their shows and, if appropriate, a link to the programme on this site. It is amazing to see how many comedies certain actors have been in, though they may be remembered for just one or two. Fascinating stuff, especially if you enjoy clicking around and browsing.

Megalinks If you've squeezed every drop of information out of this site but still want more, simply find the programme you're interested in, click it and get recommended sites dedicated to that programme.

An enormous web of painstakingly collected information. A joy for lovers of facts, figures and detail.

http://www.comedycentral.com
Comedy Central

overall rating:
★★★★★

classification:
homepage

updated:
frequently

navigation:
★★★★★

content:
★★★★

readability:
★★★★★

speed:
★★★★★

US

With over 66 million subscribers to the only television comedy network, you'd expect their website to be of a high standard, and it is. However, as it's an American company and all the content is aimed at the American market, some sections are not applicable outside the States. For instance, the section offering tickets to watch certain shows being filmed is of no use unless you're in America or planning a trip over there. Don't worry too much, though; there's loads of content, based on the programmes they show, for discerning comedy fans everywhere. The latest news runs down the bulk of the page, and the navigation links are on the left. Clicking on these takes you to a variety of excellent, well-designed pages. It's nice to look at and is updated all the time, so there's plenty of reasons to check back often.

SPECIAL FEATURES

TV Show Sites Click a programme title and you're taken to an excellent page about that show. Some are exclusively American and will be unfamiliar to anyone who doesn't watch the channel on cable or satellite. However, there are pages dedicated to South Park, The League of Gentlemen and Absolutely Fabulous and other well-known comedy programmes.

Only on the Web Waste an hour or two wandering aimlessly around this collection of exclusive web 'stuff'. There's a variety of sounds, pictures and video clips to download from some of the featured shows. You can pay to download whole episodes of South Park, which seems rather excessive. You can also have comedy radio played through your PC while you surf. There are some very funny recordings of top comedians at work and even some comedy songs. Well worth a listen. If you've got lots of time on your hands there are some unusual games to play, all rather pointless, but it's only for fun. The South Park ones are easily the best.

Official Comedy Central Store Lots of stuff to buy. It's all priced in dollars, though, so if you're not in the USA it's probably better to find and order what you want from a more local internet store.

OTHER FEATURES

News and Banter Sign up for the free newsletter, send ecards or even listen to some comedy interviews.

A very well put-together site, great to look at and with up-to-the-minute content. The only downside is the number of shows that are only known to Comedy Central Channel subscribers.

http://friends.warnerbros.com/cmp/index.html
Friends

It looks classy, has a fun atmosphere, has more content than you could ever possibly need, and gets updated pretty frequently. How many other 'official' sites can say that? The main navigation links are down the left-hand side, but don't be disappointed if this doesn't seem like a lot; wait until you see how much lies beyond them. However, you sometimes have to wait quite a long time for the pages to download. If your patience can take it though, it's worth the wait. There's also a navigation bar across the bottom of each page you visit. The only thing it misses are the obsessive lists of trivia that a lot of fan sites have. If that's what you're after, try looking at the other two Friends sites recommended in the Other Sites of Interest at the end of this chapter.

SPECIAL FEATURES

Neighbourhood This is the scenic and quirky way to get around the site. Graphically it's a wonderful representation of a high street, with a variety of buildings. Each of these buildings is a link to Friends goodies. Move your mouse along the row of buildings and short descriptions appear. Not everything available from the site can be found here, so remember to check the more mundane looking links on the main page too.

Become a Friend Sign up for the newsletter to get all the gossip and news that's not available from anywhere else.

overall rating:	★★★★★
classification:	official site
updated:	frequently
navigation:	★★★★★
content:	★★★★★
readability:	★★★★★
speed:	★★★★
US	

comedy

Today's Friends Poll Every day there's a question and your opinion is wanted. Just click your choice and come back tomorrow for the results.

Behind the Scenes Find out about the actors, watch video snippets, wander round the sets and even see a short clip of the Friends team filming in front of a live audience. This is content that only an official site could have.

Friends Gamezone Fancy yourself as an avid Friends buff? Take the test and see how much you can remember from the series in this quiz. There's a Friends version of the old card game Pairs (with limited appeal) and a great video quiz where a question is based on an event from an episode and you play the clip to see if you got the answer right.

Video Theatre Clips to download. Don't be surprised if they take a long time to load, some clips are over 6MB.

Friends Freebies Don't get too excited at the idea of Freebies, there are photos, sounds, more video clips and the odd postcard to send to your friends over the net.

There are also Message Boards and Chat rooms that can be accessed through the navigation bar at the bottom of each page.

An absolutely excellent, official site that really looks after its fans. There's everything you'd expect from a dedicated site but it's all done with more class and style than most.

http://www.haveigotnewsforyou.co.uk/cgi-bin/home.cgi
Have I Got News For You

overall rating:	★ ★ ★ ★ ★
classification:	official site
updated:	daily
navigation:	★ ★ ★ ★ ★
content:	★ ★ ★ ★ ★
readability:	★ ★ ★ ★ ★
speed:	★ ★ ★ ★ ★
UK	

This site is in the same chatty, funny style as the TV programme. It's nicely designed and easy to get around. The site has combined some of the rounds, which you can play for prizes, with some brand new features, like interviews where you can pose the questions. The site is slowly growing into something worthy of its excellent TV counterpart. There's an Anorak section with questions based on this week's show, and if you log on early on Friday you can see one of the actual Odd One Out questions from that evening's show. Phew. The personalities of the show are used to set the tone of the features, especially Angus' dry humour, whether he's had any actual involvement or not. The interactive games can be found by clicking the links at the top of the page. The competitions are updated daily, so why not make this your first stop every day?

SPECIAL FEATURES

Odd One Out Just like the round on the show, you're shown four photographs and asked to say which is the odd one out and why. You can see the answers suggested by others and vote for the one you think is right, or just funniest.

Missing Words Very simply, look at the newspaper headline and think what word might fit in the blank. You can enter as many times as you like, and don't forget to check back tomorrow and vote for your favourite. If you want to look at some previous questions, there are archives going back for months.

Caption Competition Look at the photo and create a caption for it. Once again, remember to vote for your favourite answer tomorrow.

Vote This is where you decide who came up with the funniest answers in yesterday's competitions. The winners get a T-shirt. Be warned, every single answer is there for you to judge, and there are sometimes hundreds of them.

Not very much about the show, but it's great fun to pit your wits against some questions from the show.

http://www.hookystreet.co.uk
Hooky Street

overall rating: ★★★★★
classification: fan site
updated: frequently
navigation: ★★★★★
content: ★★★★★
readability: ★★★★
speed: ★★★★★
UK

Quite simply an excellent Only Fools and Horses fan site. From the first moment you'll see that there are masses of links all over the place, so it's very easy to explore. What's more difficult is knowing where to start. The top of the central column lists all the latest newsworthy items, while recent site updates are at the top of the right-hand column. After that, it's up to you. Most of the site features are listed in the column on the left under the main headings of Information and, further down, Entertainment. Nothing is missing from this wonderful site, but I'm sure if you think of something they'd be glad to hear from you.

SPECIAL FEATURES

Episode Guide Fifteen years of Only Fools and Horses episodes. Each has a plot summary, sound and video clips and a rating. Brilliant. Brings the memories flooding back.

The Cast Brief but informative biographies of all the cast members. Peppered with fascinating insider trivia like the fact that David Jason made, on average, nearly £70,000 per episode of the show. Written in a friendly style that instantly appeals.

Merchandise Books, videos and lots of other Fools and Horses related stuff. Many of the items can be bought right here on line. There are also loads of exclusive items available from the Fan Club, just click their link.

Radio Station Popular songs from Only Fools and Horses play all day and night to entertain while you work or surf.

Quiz Every month there's a nicely presented quiz that even grades you when you're finished. Be warned, though: it's not very easy unless you're a real fan of the show, and blessed with a great memory.

Video/Audio You would expect to find clips from the show on any fan site, but this goes one step further. You can watch a variety of clips including adverts and other shows featuring the main actors.

Sound Clips Download some of the most famous one-liners from the show, then listen to the opening and closing theme music from the show.

OTHER FEATURES

There's a chat room, message board, photos, desktop themes, cartoons and competitions. If it has anything to do with Only Fools and Horses it will probably find its way onto these pages.

This site has only been around since the start of 1999, but it rates as the best Only Fools and Horses site on the web. There's loads to do and it's kept wonderfully up to date. Luvvly Jubbly.

http://s9000.furman.edu/~ejorgens/cheers/top.html
The Original Cheers Website

No longer in production and with half the cast moved on to other things, including spin-offs like Frasier, you'd think it would be hard to find anything of substance about Cheers. Then you stumble across this site and realise it's the only Cheers site you, or anyone, will ever need. It's a very simple but effectively designed site, with the accent definitely placed on informative content rather than pointless layout. It's a very easy site to get around; all the main links are boxed towards the bottom of the homepage. As with a lot of dedicated fan sites, this one started out with enormous plans which, unfortunately, have not been fulfilled. This means several sections are incomplete. Thankfully, they got some excellent work done before they went off the boil.

SPECIAL FEATURES

Episodes A break down of 269 Cheers episodes. You get the cast list and production team, a brief plot summary and cross-referenced links to the main characters and actors. You can also vote for your favourite episode.

Characters Lots of information on the main characters as well as familiar faces who popped up now and then. Each section is filled with cross-references to episodes and other characters. Unfortunately, some of the sections are not completed yet.

overall rating:	★ ★ ★ ★ ★
classification:	fan site
updated:	incomplete
navigation:	★ ★ ★ ★ ★
content:	★ ★ ★ ★
readability:	★ ★ ★ ★ ★
speed:	★ ★ ★ ★ ★

US

Actors A huge database on all the regulars and supporting actors, and even famous faces who only appeared once or twice. Again there is a wealth of cross-referencing, with links to the characters, specific episodes and even the actors' entries on the Internet Movie Database.

OTHER FEATURES

Audio Sound clips from the show are available for downloading in two different formats.

Misc Everything that didn't fit nicely somewhere else. Here you can find, amongst other things, the Cheers drinking game, lists of quotes and a wish list which seems to be redundant as the site's construction has ground to a halt.

Archives The FAQs live here, as do the lyrics to the theme song, a list of 'Normisms' and a list of awards the show won.

Feedback Got a question? Check it's not already been covered in the FAQ, fill out the form and see what they say.

The Trivia and **Guestbook** sections are currently unavailable.

A great site that ran out of steam before it was finished. It's a real shame, but it's still the best Cheers site out there.

http://members.nbci.com/mail2kramer/news.html
The Seinfeldest Site On The Web

overall rating:
★★★★★

classification:
fan site

updated:
occasionally

navigation:
★★★★★

content:
★★★★★

readability:
★★★★★

speed:
★★★★★

UK

This is the biggest Seinfeld site there is, so they claim. Unlike a lot of big sites, though, it's very simply designed and extremely easy to get around. If you scroll down from the smiley faces of the cast you find the message board and guestbook links, under which are the main navigation links for the rest of the site. Updates slowed down considerably at the start of 2000, but this is to be expected with a show that is no longer being made. The whole site has been created with the love and care of a true fan who wants to share their obsession with the world. Even if you've never seen the show, you may check out the odd re-run after being impressed by this site.

SPECIAL FEATURES

Site News News of site updates are posted here. Make sure you have a look at the News From the Final Episode link, an incredible fact-by-fact account of the weeks running up to the screening of the last ever episode in America.

Movies There are currently 38 movies to enjoy, but with some clips needing up to 10MB to download, you could be waiting some time before you watch them.

Seinfeld Sounds At the last count there were over 200 sound files to download. Each file is neatly presented with a brief description of what you're getting. There are also compilations of funny clips and links to the players you need to listen to them.

Scripts There are more than 30 full episode scripts plus a couple of episodes that never made it onto the TV. Typical of the site is this helpful touch: a link to another Seinfeld site with even more scripts, should you want them.

The Characters This is where a huge library of cast photos is stored. Click on the faces at the top of the page to go to a brief biography and lots of pictures.

Cool Extras The all-important episode guide, Seinfeld's sex dictionary, and the option to generate a different final episode description if you didn't like the one they showed or if you just fancy a laugh.

OTHER FEATURES

Seinfeld Links If you think you need more Seinfeld stuff after this one, you may need medical attention rather than this brilliantly presented list of other sites, with reviews and ratings.

Seinfeld Store Mostly links to online companies selling related merchandise.

Screensavers Love 'em or hate 'em, here's another seven to add to your collection. Some of them have to be reinstalled every five times they're played, which is ridiculous.

Seinfeld has gone but will live on forever with sites like this, which take being a fan way over and above the call of duty.

http://www.btinternet.com/~c.tomlinson/fawlty.htm
The Unofficial Guide to Fawlty Towers

overall rating:	★★★★★
classification:	fan site
updated:	regularly
navigation:	★★★★★
content:	★★★★★
readability:	★★★★★
speed:	★★★★★
UK	

Fawlty Towers was recently voted number one in the top 100 British TV programmes of all time, and quite rightly so. What is unusual about Fawlty Towers on the internet is that you can still get an up-to-date site dedicated to a series that ended more than 20 years ago. Right from the first page there are links to all the latest news surrounding the show and its stars. Navigation is only slightly complicated by the sheer weight of material on the site. The left-hand frame contains five 'floors' and 'grounds' filled with interesting stuff, and it's always there wherever you go in the site. It's not terribly inspiring to look at, preferring to keep it simple and let the content speak for itself.

SPECIAL FEATURES

First Floor The links under this heading are fairly self-explanatory. You can Search Our Site, check out the History of the series and how the idea came about, sign the Guest Book or leave a posting on the Message Board and find loads more Links to sites and articles. There's even a noughts and crosses game.

Second Floor This is where the Fawlty Towers Quiz lives, with 10 multiple choice questions and a comment on how you did. The rest of the floor is dedicated to news and reviews and articles about the American version of Fawlty Towers, called Payne.

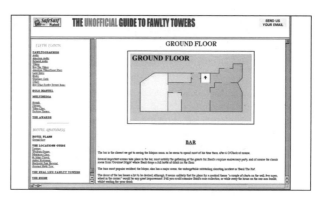

Third Floor Read the Episode Guides, which contain cast lists and plot outlines. There's a link to another site where you can search TV listings to see if and when the show will be televised next. Finally, there's a View From a Torquay Hotel Bedroom Window, and why not?

Fourth Floor There are brief Biographies of all the leading and some of the supporting cast members. Where appropriate there are links to videos and recordings featuring the actor, and a link to other sites featuring them. There's also a brief discussion on why the hotel has so few employees and some trivia about three actors who appeared in the series twice, as different characters.

Fifth Floor There has been a wealth of Fawlty Towers merchandise, and on this floor you can both read about it and follow links to where some of the items can be bought. For Manuel fans there is also a quite detailed section on Andrew Sachs' use of the Manuel character outside of Fawlty Towers, in adverts, on stage and in the future. There is also the Multimedia section, which, apart from a handful of photos, is a series of links to other sites that house sound files, video clips and more photos still. And finally, what no self-respecting Fawlty Towers fan should be without on their computer – Desktop Themes and screensavers.

Hotel Grounds For the Fawlty Towers fan who wants trivia over and above the call of duty. Firstly, you can check out the ground plans of the hotel. You can also read some details about the actual locations mentioned in the show, from Torquay itself to André's Restaurant which was used in the episode called Gourmet Night. There are even little sections on palm trees in Torquay and hotels that have actually called themselves Fawlty Towers.

A superb site for fans of the show, with not just a bit of this and that but a lot of everything. It will also keep growing, so check back often.

overall rating: ★ ★ ★ ★ ★
classification: fan site
updated: frequently
navigation: ★ ★ ★ ★ ★
content: ★ ★ ★ ★ ★
readability: ★ ★ ★ ★ ★
speed: ★ ★ ★ ★ ★
UK

http://www.whispersfromwalmington.com
Whispers From Walmington (Dad's Army)

Don't think for one second that you'll spend just a few minutes strolling through here. You'll need sandwiches, a flask, your sleeping bag and a week off work to get the full benefit of this huge site. Rather than putting lots of only vaguely related items together under umbrella headings, Dave Coventry, who started the site in August 1999, has kept everything separate and under individual headings – hence the lengthy list running down the left of the page. You can pick and choose from this list or click the Next button at the top of each page, which will take you through the sections alphabetically. It's a friendly site, with the overall feel of a wonderfully maintained scrapbook which is constantly being added to and improved. You are invited to get involved, sending any information you can to improve the site.

SPECIAL FEATURES

What's New There's so much going on here, this is probably the best place to come if you're dropping by for the second time or more. All the updates are listed chronologically, and items that are new since you personally visited the site last have a special marker.

Anorak Stuff Quote things from this page to non fans of the programme and they'll become a little nervous. Only maniacally devoted fans need shooting locations, vehicle descriptions (with registration plate numbers), and an ever-growing list on bloopers sent in by eagle-eyed viewers. There are also links to another anorak site, and to yet another Dad's Army site run by the same guy!

Appreciation Society Dad's Army fans are not alone. For £6 you can join the society, receive quarterly newsletters and buy special merchandise.

DAAS Convention 2000 If you want to know what the appreciation society gets up to, check these great photos taken at the convention.

Articles of War This section is set to grow and grow. Visitors are invited to send in anecdotes and stories with a Dad's Army theme. There are already articles on rationing, life during the war and some photos from the period.

Episode Guide Brief plot outlines for every episode from all nine series.

Greetings Cards Create and send your very own Dad's Army cards over the net.

Main Characters A photo and a little background on the main characters.

Sounds A large and growing collection of famous and funny sound clips from the show.

Theme Song You just know you've got to have it. All the words are here and several versions of the song are available to download, including one you can put on your mobile phone.

Whispers Mailing Lists Be kept in touch with all things Dad's Army or sign up for an updates email.

OTHER FEATURES

Audio Cassettes, Books, and Videos includes details of what you can buy and where to get it online. The Gallery contains over 1,300 images. Click Screen Saver and Theme to brighten up your computer with some Dad's Army alterations.

This is an incredible site, and it promises to grow into one of the best fan sites on the internet.

http://www.yesminister.demon.nl
Yes Minister Homepage

A very informative and detailed site dedicated to both Yes Minister and Yes Prime Minister. It has a clutter-free design, with site links on the left and the content in the main frame. From the front page you get brief descriptions of what to expect as you browse the site. Although the shows are no longer being made the site is still updated fairly frequently.

SPECIAL FEATURES

Introduction Brief reminder about the show, its plot and airing dates.

Episodes Nearly every episode has a detailed plot description and transcripts of the top five funny moments from each episode, which can be downloaded.

Database Includes details of every person appearing or mentioned in the show, whether they're real or fictional. It also includes details about institutions, governmental terms, places and abbreviations mentioned in either series. It's a very comprehensive section.

Video/Books Rather than just a list, this is a useful page advising you on the current state of video availability. There's also a large list of links if you're looking to buy.

Vote/Results Join in with other fans and have your say about the programmes and this site, then see the results section, to see

overall rating:
★ ★ ★ ★ ★

classification:
fan site

updated:
frequently

navigation:
★ ★ ★ ★ ★

content:
★ ★ ★ ★ ★

readability:
★ ★ ★ ★ ★

speed:
★ ★ ★ ★ ★

NE

what everyone else thought. The results are presented in an election-night style, with lots of pie charts and statistics.

OTHER FEATURES

Photos Some very similar pictures, mostly group shots of the main characters. Not of a high quality.

Music Very tinny version of the theme music, which loops until you're sick of it, which won't be long.

Download There's a desktop theme, a screen saver and a game that was written for the Commodore 64 which you need an emulator for.

Lots of content, lots of detail, and not afraid to ask you what you'd like to see added or changed. This is one fan site that will definitely last.

http://www.pythonline.com
Pythonline

A very nicely designed site. After clicking Continue on the front page, you're bombarded with Python style cartoons. Wave your mouse around and a far more civilised pop-up box tells you what to expect when you start clicking. Once you're inside, the same links are available at the top of each new page. As with many 'official' sites, the designers have left out what lots of fans like to see and collect. There are no photo, sound or video sections and some of the content is pointless in the extreme. However, the pages have exactly the right Python 'feel', and you can't be a proper fan without checking out the official site, can you? Every now and then some kind soul even updates a few bits, so you can't complain.

SPECIAL FEATURES

New Stuff If any of the Pythons are up to something, you'll find the details of it here. Cleese has been writing, and Idle has both made a new TV programme and been touring with his one-man show.

The Spam Club You can change your horoscope in a less than funny feature, or send abuse to those you love most dearly, in the form of a mildly amusing pick-and-mix email message. To join the club, follow the links. It's not actually a Monty Python Club, but part of a much bigger network which sends you information about lots of celebs.

overall rating:
★ ★ ★ ★

classification:
official site

updated:
occasionally

navigation:
★ ★ ★ ★ ★

content:
★ ★ ★ ★

readability:
★ ★ ★ ★ ★

speed:
★ ★ ★ ★ ★

UK

Plugs Supposedly written by John Cleese, although that's open to question. You will find not one single fact to entertain your friends with. However, if you want very funny parodies of Python team biographies as well as ridiculous fact-fiction about their lives and work, read on. Very funny. Very clever. Just what you expect from one of the funniest writing teams of all time. You'll also find links to other related sites.

Shopping Loads of great stuff to buy; unfortunately, it all ships from America, so has added shipping costs.

OTHER FEATURES

De Tour An almost unnecessary guide to the website in the almost capable hands of Daphne, ex-lap-dancer and fan of the shopping page. She tells you, very briefly, what to expect when you click, but is really nothing more than site padding.

Chit Chat Not a chat room but a bulletin board. Actually, make that a series of bulletin boards. Although each board's name is dedicated to an individual Python, the content is varied and based on anything. Anyone can read the messages, but you have to register to reply, which is free after you have filled out an online form. They're busy boards, with lots of posts a week.

There's lots and yet, at the same time, very little here. Dedicated Python fans will love it. Others may be left wondering if it's finished.

http://www.geocities.com/Paris/2694/craggy.html
The Craggy Island Examiner

With the death of Dermot Morgan in 1998, many Father Ted websites soon ground to an understandable halt. However, The Craggy Island Examiner still remains a superb resource for Father Ted fans even though it is now seldom updated. The style is very simple and plain, each page looks like it has been written on concrete, but with 24 sections clickable from the boxes on the front page, there's plenty to keep you interested. Below are the best bits.

SPECIAL FEATURES

FEQ An appropriately titled page for Frequently Asked Questions. It's a huge list and loads of areas of information are covered. Very comprehensive if you're desperately looking for an answer, and just a good read if you're not.

Quotes Loads and loads of great quotes. They might not be quite so funny if you don't know the characters' voices, but if you don't, what are you doing here?

TedSpotting A fairly comprehensive list of what the Father Ted actors have appeared in, both before and after Craggy Island.

Priests Only for the crazed, obsessive fan. List of priests, real and imaginary, that have been mentioned on the show. Too much detail for mere mortals.

overall rating:	★ ★ ★ ★
classification:	fan site
updated:	rarely
navigation:	★ ★ ★ ★ ★
content:	★ ★ ★ ★
readability:	★ ★ ★ ★
speed:	★ ★ ★ ★ ★
UK	

Sounds Some excellent files. Just click on the links to hear some of the most memorable one-liners from the series.

Episode Guide Every Father Ted episode with its original showing date, a brief plot summary and an appropriate quote.

OTHER FEATURES

Morgue A collection of articles and interviews about Father Ted, its actors and its subject matter.

Theme Easily download the series theme in a number of different formats.

Fan Fiction Views are mixed on the worth of fan fiction. Even the Father Ted writers think time might be better spent trying to write and sell original material. But, if you like to read what others think might have happened in Father Ted, here's your chance.

Pictures Every fan site has them and here they are. A couple of dozen scans and video grabs of varying size and quality.

Trivia Quiz Thirty-five questions to see if you've been watching carefully. If you're not a fan, prepare to do badly.

The site was never intended to be an up-to-the-minute news service for the show and its actors, more an encyclopaedia of fan-based information. At this, it very definitely succeeds.

http://www.tvgohome.com/index.html
TV Go Home

'Don't be tasteless without also being imaginative', say the guidelines for submitting ideas to this adult parody of the Radio Times. Maybe it should also point out that writing that drips with aggressive, know-it-all angst can seem like complete pants after a while. Each issue of TV Go Home features a single page of TV listings. The content is hit and miss, very often relying on strong language and descriptions of violence over any real comedy ideas. However, when it's funny it's brutally so. The weekly review of a prime time show featuring Nathan Barley is always funny and often quite brilliantly written with enough acid to fill several oversized baths.

If you think the world is filled with zombie-like people who are completely removed from reality, and you'd like to see them, at the very least, horribly ridiculed, then you will undoubtedly sign up for this fortnightly dose of gratuitous satire. It's worth it.

SPECIAL FEATURES

Front Page This week's issue in all its glory.

Archives More copies going back to March 1999.

Suggestions Think you can do better? TV Go Home want to see your ideas. Read the guidelines first and be prepared to give up all rights to your ideas the minute you post them off.

overall rating:	★ ★ ★ ★
classification:	homepage
updated:	fortnightly
navigation:	★ ★ ★ ★ ★
content:	★ ★ ★ ★
readability:	★ ★ ★ ★ ★
speed:	★ ★ ★ ★ ★
UK 18	

Subscribe   Rather than getting your inbox filled with large emails, every two weeks you'll simply get a reminder that there is a new copy online. Sign up now.

FAQ   As always, this is the first place to look if you want to understand more about the mind behind the site.

Not for the faint-hearted, language wise, but filled with clever satire even though the laughs are sometimes questionable.

http://www.mrbean.co.uk
The Official Mr Bean Website

There's lots going on at this website. It's all written by the usually silent Mr Bean himself, so it is suitably silly. Some of the features are nothing more than an excuse to pad the site out and make it appear crammed with goodies, but it soon becomes painfully obvious that the site was created to cash in on the successful film and sell lots of merchandise. That said, to the younger visitor it may be a fun and exciting experience. It's certainly a colourful site with lots of graphics, but this makes some of the pages a bit lethargic when loading. The main links are in the left-hand frame, in red, or you can click on teddy in the bottom left corner to go to his very own page. Click on any of them and the new page opens in the right frame. Links within this page are at the top of it. It's unclear whether the site is ever updated, but I suspect not.

SPECIAL FEATURES

Fun Lab Not great. Mr Bean tries to write a dictionary of only useful words, but gets bored after the letter A. Then he tries to tell you about some wonderful sites, including Shirley Bassey's homepage and a clickable link to a fictitious cheese page. There are also sections dedicated to Mr Bean's inventions and some cartoon 'remote cameras'.

Bean: The Movie Excellent section dedicated to the movie, including plot details, photos, video clips and assorted silliness.

overall rating:	★ ★ ★
classification:	official site
updated:	uncertain
navigation:	★ ★ ★ ★ ★
content:	★ ★ ★
readability:	★ ★ ★ ★
speed:	★ ★ ★ ★
UK	

Mr Bean Online Store At last, the reason why the site's here. You can buy loads of Bean-related items and get a free poster with every order.

OTHER FEATURES

All About Me Not a biography but where Mr Bean tells us, amongst other things, about the two uses of the knee, which are 'bendy' and 'straight'. Daft rather than funny.

Millennium Bean Oh dear, oh dear, oh dear; someone forgot to take their funny pill when they designed this page, and their 'have a point' and 'make it interesting' pills too.

Mr Bean Official Fan Club The page tells you of lots of goodies you get for becoming a member, but the link to Buy doesn't work – and at nearly £13 it's probably just as well. However, you can also get membership from the online store section where the link still works.

Teddy Page Teddy's designed his own page, where children's drawings are displayed and little else.

If you're honest about the site, you have to admit it's simply a way to sell Mr Bean merchandise. It's probably aimed at younger fans, but I suspect even they may be a little disappointed.

http://www.abfab.demon.nl
Global Absolutely Fabulous Site

There is a wacky feel to the site, with psychedelic backgrounds
to the pages keeping everything in the style of the series.
There's a lot of ground covered, with a lot of sections to browse,
but the site never really goes far enough. It's as though it never
got finished and had to be content with some padding to make
it long enough. Which is a real shame as there are some nice
features. Unless the rumoured new series ever materialises it's
unlikely there will be much in the way of updates. Pity.

SPECIAL FEATURES

Fab Faq A pretty detailed Frequently Asked Questions section.
However, some of the questions seem a little unnecessary, like
'Is Saffy a Virgin?'. If you really need to know, the answers are all
there.

Life Style Eddy and Patsy talk brand names throughout each
episode; here are some links to the actual places they mention.
Not comic but interesting.

Characters If you're not sure who someone is, look here, and be
in the dark no longer.

Episode Guide This takes you straight to the part of the Fab Faq
which lists each episode with a very brief plot line.

Trivia Challenge Answer the AbFab trivia and let Patsy tell you if
you're right or wrong.

overall rating:	★ ★ ★
classification:	fan site
updated:	not
navigation:	★ ★ ★ ★ ★
content:	★ ★ ★
readability:	★ ★ ★ ★ ★
speed:	★ ★ ★ ★
US	

OTHER FEATURES

AbFab Videos and News Hugely disappointing section of the site. The news is horribly out of date and the links to videos take you to the American version of Amazon, where all the titles are currently not available. If you want to buy AbFab videos, try the site at Amazon.co.uk.

Fabulous Things A collection of things that don't fit anywhere else. There's a nice signed photo of Joanna Lumley, an early review of the site and an almost academic conversation about the series, its themes and background.

With a much better design than a lot of fan sites, it's such a shame the content on here isn't of the same standard.

OTHER SITES OF INTEREST

Ab Fab Splurge

http://www.comedycentral.com/splurge

Become Edina or Patsy and take your $5000 in virtual cash and go on the shopping spree of a lifetime in this Comedy Central game. You choose what you buy and try to accumulate fashion points, but be careful, buy the wrong things and your fashionable reputation will take a plunge. A simply daft game which fans of Absolutely Fabulous will simply adore, sweetie.

American Comedy on British TV

http://www.geocities.com/TelevisionCity/7916/bandex.html

This is really nothing more than a jazzed-up list of links. However, it covers a lot of American shows. Every show page also has some photos. Just to make sure there's no bias, there is also a huge section dedicated to British Comedy on American TV and another to Essential Afro Centric Comedy, which covers links to essentially black comedy series.

British Comedy Wavs

http://www.geocities.com/TelevisionCity/Stage/5786/wavs.html

Do you love situation comedies, but sometimes get fed up just reading about them? Why not download some clips from your favourite shows, put them on your computer or just play them over and over? There's a good selection of famous programmes and lots of sound clips here. For convenience, a zip file is supplied, containing all the clips for a particular show.

There's also a link to the amusing British Cultural References page, which explains things that Americans might not understand in British comedy; like, who Danny La Rue is, and what exactly you get if you have a Curly Wurly.

Friends
http://www.friends-tv.org

A good fan site, well worth looking at in conjunction with the Official Friends site. There's an excellent and absorbing Frequently Asked Questions section, and a huge episode guide with plot summaries and quotes for every single Friends episode. There's masses of information about the music used in the show, and you can even get complete scripts for every episode. If this isn't enough there are links to other Friends sites, newsgroups and mailing lists.

Friends Newsletters
http://members.aol.com/Settember/Frnews.html

Keep in touch with all the news and gossip about the show, the characters and the actors. There are currently more than 6000 fans enjoying this excellent weekly newsletter. And it's absolutely free, so what are you waiting for? Even if you don't fancy the newsletters there's absolutely loads of information, facts and trivia about everything to do with Friends. It's updated all the time too. Excellent site, well worth a look.

Radio Times Comedy Zone
http://www.comedyzone.beeb.com

The BBC can be very proud of this excellent portal for comedy.

There are links to all sorts of specially created sites dedicated to shows from Are you Being Served to Shooting Stars. There's fantastic advice for would-be comedy writers, lots of features that change often so there's always something new to see, and even Fun and Games and weekly columns to keep you entertained. While you're at it, why not join the webclub for weekly e-mails and special offers? All in all, it's a great site for a wide variety of comedy.

Saturday Net
http://www.io.com/~serpas/snl.html
Saturday Night Live launched the careers of dozens of today's top comedy actors, including Dan Aykroyd, Eddie Murphy, Billy Crystal, Mike Myers and Adam Sandler. It has been running for more than 25 years, and this site is a very basic but huge database of every episode and every performer who ever graced the show. It's sometimes a little difficult to follow, because with so much information crammed into one place there are lots of abbreviations and list conventions to remember. However, it's a list and trivia lover's dream.

The Unofficial Monty Python Homepage
http://www.mwscomp.com/python.html
A series of very tinny Python songs play here; however, once you're into the crazy Python world, the quality doesn't seem to matter. It hasn't been updated for quite a while, but there's lots of songs and a selection of scripts on offer, although that makes the site seem a little defunct given that you can buy the complete scripts in one big volume from good book shops. Still,

there is a great section on the Python films and lots of links to related Monty madness. It's slightly thrown together, as many fan sites are, but there's lots to make your visit worthwhile.

TV Corner

http://www.tvcorner-online.com

Very simply, this is a huge listings site for websites connected to TV subjects: actors, episode guides, official sites, FAQs, merchandise, and that's just for starters. Each link has a brief description of what to expect if you pay the site a visit and a rather unused rating system, which relies on you giving your opinion. Nearly all the sites are American based, but there's a search facility so you can more easily find something specific of interest.

cinema

Humour in films must be one of the most subjective elements in the world of comedy. So many 'funny' films are made that barely raise a smile, or are simply the repetition of tired and worn-out devices that we've all seen before.

The internet, however, has its ways of clinging on to the really funny films and the best comedy actors. Fans put them on pedestals for the rest of us to take note. Some of those sites are covered in this chapter. Even if you disagree with some of the choices, because you don't consider the subject matter to your humour tastes, you have to admire the huge amounts of hard work that have gone into creating these pages.

And if you hate these sites, hate films, hate comedy and received this guide as a present you never wanted, why not check out The Golden Raspberries site, which covers all that's awful in cinema. You'll probably feel right at home.

comedy

overall rating:	★ ★ ★ ★ ★
classification:	official site
updated:	not
navigation:	★ ★ ★ ★
content:	★ ★ ★ ★ ★
readability:	★ ★ ★ ★ ★
speed:	★ ★ ★ ★
US	

http://www.austinpowers.com
Austin Powers

Even if you didn't like the films too much, you have to admire the website. Filled to overflowing with photos, psychedelic graphics, sound clips and features, there's so much to do that it's difficult to know where to start. Everything on the front page moves and changes, so before you get hypnotised, click on one of the faces to go to a new section, which opens with a Flash introduction that you can skip if you've already seen it. These front page links are also available down the left of each subsequent page. If you're more interested in the first film, click on Back In Time in the white box halfway down the page, for the original site. Unless there's another Powers film, this site is unlikely to be updated, so simply enjoy it while you can.

SPECIAL FEATURES

Auction Powers Click on the big winking Austin face and you're taken to a cinema auction page. It's got no real relevance to the film, but it obviously provides the sponsorship for the site. You can, however, find some incredible things to bid for, including actual props from actual films. Content changes all the time, so you'll need a good browse.

Austin All the usual fan stuff like photos, screensavers, sound bites and wallpaper. You can also play interactive Austin Powers stories and download a clever-sounding speaking clock that, when unzipped, refused to work. Typical.

Evil If evil is your thing, vote for which minion should die before you check out more photos, sounds and an evil screensaver.

Shag So many girls, so little time. Vote for your favourite babe, then download yet more wallpaper, photos and another screensaver featuring the girls.

OTHER FEATURES

At the top of each section are some links directly related to the films.

Cast Excellent biographies of all the main actors.

Production Detailed background to the film. Very interesting and informative.

Excellent place for Austin Powers fans; other film pages could take notes on how a good film site should look.

comedy

overall rating: ★★★★★	
classification: guide	
updated: frequently	
navigation: ★★★★	
content: ★★★★	
readability: ★★★★★	
speed: ★★★★★	
UK	

http://www.britmovie.co.uk/index.html
Brit Movie

This is a dedicated reference site to British movies. It covers all genres of British movies, not just comedy from, early black and white to current blockbusters. Navigation is slightly complicated as the different sections have slightly different names, depending on where you look. For simplicity use the drop-down menu at the top of the page.

SPECIAL FEATURES

Film Genres There are 12 genres to choose from, with the Comedy link in the bottom left-hand corner. Click this and you're faced with an alphabetical list of all the British films covered. Each links to a synopsis of the film, cast and production credits. If appropriate you will also find links to Images from the film and places to buy the video. It's by no means a complete list of films, but the content is good for the featured movies.

Forum This is actually 16 message boards, each dedicated to a different topic. So if your interest is General Film Chat or more especially about your Favourite British Film, there's a specific board. Postings are not fast and furious, but it is unusual for a message to receive no replies.

Trying to cover such a huge topic as the British film industry is a huge task, but this ever-growing site seems to be up for the challenge.

http://www.geocities.com/Hollywood/Screen/7157/chaplin/chaplin.html
Charlie Chaplin UK

A very attractively designed site, dedicated to one of cinema's very first comedy actors. It reads like a nice coffee table book, with quality photos and sensitively written pages that have a more mature ring than most internet fan sites. Little bits and pieces are added fairly frequently, and a few major changes are in the pipeline. The main links are on the front page, either side of the smallish photo of Chaplin. Don't click the main headings themselves, click on the blue text underneath. A few other links are in the rectangle underneath.

SPECIAL FEATURES

Ographies As well as a brief biography, there's also a superb Chronology of Charlie Chaplin's life, detailing every year. As well as covering what was going on in his life, it also looks at the world of cinema and the world at large. It's absolutely fascinating and worth the visit to the site all by itself. The People Index link takes you to details of all his major leading ladies, his family and friends and the people who worked with him at The Mutual Company. Very informative and nicely laid out.

UK Guide This covers where you can find Chaplin on the television, at the cinema, and details of his videos that are available to buy.

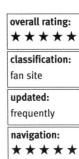

overall rating:
★ ★ ★ ★ ★

classification:
fan site

updated:
frequently

navigation:
★ ★ ★ ★ ★

content:
★ ★ ★ ★ ★

readability:
★ ★ ★ ★ ★

speed:
★ ★ ★ ★

UK

Exhibition Hall Posters, photos, Contemporary Promotions and advertisements that have used Chaplin in their campaigns. There are even photos of his grave.

Articles A selection of articles that range from a radio transcript to Chaplin quotes and his famous Great Dictator speech.

Edna Section dedicated to Edna Purviance, one of Chaplin's early leading ladies.

Books Details of Chaplin books and links to where they can be bought online.

A wonderfully warm dedication to one of the first geniuses of comedy cinema.

http://www.jimcarreyonline.com/index.html
Jim Carrey Online

He's very famous, very rich, very funny and has a very loyal army
of fans who have created dozens of websites dedicated to him.
What makes this one stand out is that, it is also very nicely and
professionally designed, making it easy and quick to get
around. The latest news is on the front page, but you really need
to explore the links in the yellow area on the left to get a feel for
just how detailed this site is.

SPECIAL FEATURES

Movie Area Excellent section detailing Jim Carrey's films. The
content is superb, and slightly different for each film. There are
photos, video clips, production notes, cast lists and some
fascinating interviews with people who worked on the films.
There are even links to all the official sites, so you have no
excuse for not becoming a world expert.

Fan Area All the usual: a message board, chat room,
memorabilia, but what's especially nice is that they've
recognised that loads of fans would love a signed photograph
but don't really know how to go about getting one. So, there's a
step-by-step guide, right down to envelope size, on how to get
Jim's autograph.

Carrey Sightings Have you ever met the rubber-faced one
yourself? These people have and they don't mind telling you.

overall rating:	★ ★ ★ ★ ★
classification:	fan site
updated:	frequently
navigation:	★ ★ ★ ★ ★
content:	★ ★ ★ ★ ★
readability:	★ ★ ★ ★ ★
speed:	★ ★ ★ ★ ★
US	

Jim's Co-stars You've watched Jim working with some great actors and you want to know more about them? Click their photo for a fairly detailed page of information.

Bloopers You don't often see this feature on a fan site, so it's especially interesting to read the continuity mistakes, some of which even have a video clip of the offending moment.

OTHER FEATURES

Amongst other things, download all the usual stuff for your PC, check out the FAQ, see details of magazine features, and get more pictures, video and sound clips than you can cope with.

So well put together that it's interesting to real fans and casual browsers alike.

http://www.laurel-and-hardy.com/index1.html
Laurel and Hardy

As the short theme tune plays and the sepia site appears, you can feel the cinematic history in this wonderfully detailed and intelligent site. It is aimed less at the 'fan' and more at the 'connoisseur'. There's lots of background and it's nice to see a site that doesn't simply increase its page content by having loads of adverts and links everywhere. On the opening page, the site links are rather clumsily spread out, from top to bottom, but once you're into any section, the links line up far more formally on the left of the screen. There are lots of sections that give you historical information as well as just theatrical trivia about the two actors. Very comprehensive.

SPECIAL FEATURES

Hot News This is called Specials from the front page but Hot News from everywhere else. Although the duo may no longer be around, that doesn't mean there isn't news to be had. Stay up to date with this very informative news feature.

Features and Shorts It's what they're famous for. Everything Laurel and Hardy appeared in. Click the type of production you're interested in and the first, alphabetically, appears on the screen with a cast list, a photo and a brief synopsis. Other films are available from the drop-down box and other parts of this section can now be accessed by clicking the links at the top of the page.

overall rating:	★ ★ ★ ★ ★
classification:	official site
updated:	regularly
navigation:	★ ★ ★ ★ ★
content:	★ ★ ★ ★ ★
readability:	★ ★ ★ ★ ★
speed:	★ ★ ★ ★
US	

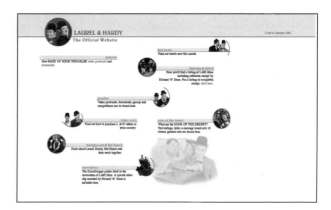

Goodies Send a classy Laurel and Hardy ecard, download video clips, and enter a competition. Also check out the Gossip section, which has a fascinating, recent question-and-answer session with Stan Laurel's daughter, Lois. It's one-offs like this that make this site really special.

Sons of the Desert A huge network of groups dedicated to Laurel and Hardy. So many, there has to be one not too far away from you. It may surprise you how popular Laurel and Hardy still are.

There's lots of background information and lots of ongoing news. It really feels like you've walked into a wonderful, cobweb-free museum rather than a website.

http://ibn-khouri.com/rwilliams
The Ultimate Robin Williams Website

Quite unusually, this site has chosen to concentrate on the work of Robin Williams rather than the man's background and private life. This was a definite choice, the reasons for which you can find in the FAQ section. That aside, it is a wonderful fan site. Firstly, it's huge, and growing all the time. Secondly, it's nicely designed. And thirdly, it has a friendly yet informative tone that makes the pages enjoyable to read without coming across as ill-informed. Basically, the design has three frames. At the top of the page are the navigation links. Don't forget to scroll down using the bar in the very top right hand corner, or you'll miss a whole row of links you can't see initially. The long thin frame on the left has all the subheadings for whichever section you've entered and the rest of the page has the detailed content. It's just undergone a huge facelift and some sections are still under construction, but it's still so good that if you were a celebrity you'd be happy to have your site presented by this guy.

SPECIAL FEATURES

Older Projects All his films, TV and theatre performances as well as relevant recordings. Each of these subheadings on the left can be clicked to bring up a cast list, plot summary, photos and any links worth looking at. Excellent record of Williams' career.

Recent Stuff This is where you'll find the most recent news of films and other projects.

overall rating:	★ ★ ★ ★ ★
classification:	fan site
updated:	regularly
navigation:	★ ★ ★ ★ ★
content:	★ ★ ★ ★ ★
readability:	★ ★ ★ ★ ★
speed:	★ ★ ★ ★ ★
US	

Future Plans Details of current projects, films that he's in talks about and so many rumoured plans that the writer must have access to some insider information. If you have any details you're invited to send them along.

Galleries There are going to be sound, video and picture galleries, but they are all currently under construction and unavailable.

FAQ Not a big section, but maybe people don't ask many questions.

Excellent on Robin Williams' career. If you want more on his personal life, you'll need to look elsewhere.

http://inspectorclouseau.com/pinkpanther
Inspector Clouseau

Surely one of the most easily recognised, most often impersonated and best loved comedy characters ever. Every Christmas, Easter and any other holiday, expect to see at least one of the Pink Panther series on a TV near you. This site is dedicated to the memory of the hapless detective, and will have funny memories flooding back in seconds. It's well organised and loads quickly. Some links run across the top of the page, but these are incomplete. In order not to miss anything, use the links at the bottom instead. These turn up on every page to make navigation even easier. Sadly, the site is no longer updated, but plenty was achieved before the creative wheels ground to a halt.

SPECIAL FEATURES
Disguises These are the results of a survey taken in 1997 to determine the favourite of Clouseau's many disguises. The list is long, and many of the suggestions have a video clip of the particular character.

Films No plot summaries or cast lists or background information. Odd for a fan site. However, there are some video clips from each film.

Lines Again, these were voted for in the 1997 survey. There are dozens of brilliantly funny lines transcribed, some of which have sound and video clips.

overall rating:	★ ★ ★ ★
classification:	fan site
updated:	not
navigation:	★ ★ ★ ★ ★
content:	★ ★ ★ ★
readability:	★ ★ ★ ★ ★
speed:	★ ★ ★ ★ ★
UK	

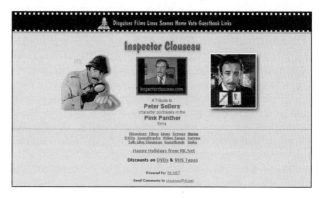

Talk Like Clouseau Fun feature. If you're going to talk like the inspector, make sure you get it just right. Eight rules to make sure Clouseau's language lives on correctly for many years to come.

This is a good Clouseau site, but if the initial aims had been realised it would surely have become great. Still, it's a fitting dedication to a brilliant comic creation.

http://www.stevemartin.net
Steve Martin

overall rating:
★ ★ ★ ★

classification:
official site

updated:
regularly

navigation:
★ ★ ★ ★ ★

content:
★ ★ ★ ★

readability:
★ ★ ★ ★ ★

speed:
★ ★ ★ ★

US

A seriously well-designed site that looks great but sometimes feels as though it's only scratching the surface rather than giving you the whole story. However, Steve Martin himself backs the site, and although he's not actively involved in the running of it, he does pop by to see how things are going. Read his comments about the site by clicking the Forward link just under the site heading. The only downside is that quality designed sites take that much longer to load each page. This one is sometimes a little sluggish.

However, it's easy to get around. The main links are the stylish buttons at the bottom of each page, with neat graphics popping up when your mouse is in the right place. Before you start clicking, though, check out the length and breadth of the opening page. Awash with detailed news, information and updates, it's one of the best sections of the site.

SPECIAL FEATURES

Films On the left are the films themselves, starting with the most recent, and on the right is a very interesting essay detailing his film career, which starts with the oldest first. It would have been nice if you could read about Steve's career and then find the links to his film right there. When you do click on a film link you're taken to a page filled with reviews of the film sent in by fans, which means there isn't much in the way of criticism.

Print Some of Steve's short essays and stories are available to read. The rest of the section simply lists the contents of Steve's published works.

Television Brief details of every time Steve Martin has appeared on television, including interviews and episodes of Saturday Night Live.

FYI An all-too-brief biography which leaves you wanting more. There are also contact details and a list of the awards Steve's won over the years.

Messages A fairly busy notice board for all things related to Steve Martin.

A really good introduction to a great comic actor, but some sections grab your interest then lose it due to a lack of depth in the content.

http://www.razzies.com/default1.asp
The Golden Raspberry Award Foundation

Have you ever seen a film that was so bad it was funny? Unfortunately, bad films do get made. Fortunately, the Golden Raspberry Foundation doesn't let them get away with it. Every year members take a vote and award the least coveted awards in the film world, The Razzies, to the very worst films and actors of the previous year. The site itself is a jumble of colour, written in a horrible font which is hard to read and not very eye-catching. The site is not up to date either, which makes you want to send a raspberry to the webmaster.

SPECIAL FEATURES

Membership Information First the bad news. If you want to be able to vote in the Razzies and take advantage of Chats, Special offers, and the rest, you'll have to join, which costs $25. Don't worry though, there's still quite a lot going on for non-members.

Razzie History and Archives Obviously, while you're here you have to check out which sorry losers have been picked out as being truly dreadful. The awards began in 1980 with Neil Diamond picking up a Worst Actor award and currently end with Bruce Willis and all the Spice Girls picking up awards in 1998.

A wonderful idea, that with 20 years of history could do with a much, much better website.

overall rating:	★ ★ ★
classification:	official site
updated:	infrequently
navigation:	★ ★ ★ ★ ★
content:	★ ★ ★
readability:	★ ★ ★
speed:	★ ★ ★ ★ ★
UK	

OTHER SITES OF INTEREST

Fansites.com
http://www.fansites.com

If you want information on a specific comedy actor, then the perfect place to begin your search is right here with Fansites. Ignore the adverts and the playstation games, the links you want are right at the top. Click either Actors or Actresses and you're taken to an alphabet page. Annoyingly, the names are arranged by first name, but click on the letter you want and sift through the dozens of actors you've never heard of until you find the one you want. Click on their name and follow the links to further links till you finally get to a site you want. There's a lot of clicking to do, but it's much more organised than simply using a search engine.

Movie Wavs
http://www.moviewavs.com/javalist.shtml

Fans of movies will collect anything, including sound bites from their favourite films. Once you've got them, you can simply keep them in a slightly 'I'm an obsessed fan' kind of way, or apply them to your computer in an 'I'm an obsessed fan and I want everyone else to know too' kind of way. Whichever you are, this is the place to start. From the first page, choose a film from the huge mountain of titles in the white box. This then takes you to a whole list of sites featuring clips from your chosen film. So, if you want Richard E. Grant screaming something obscene from Withnail and I or something frighteningly funny from Scream every time you switch the PC on, you'll find it here.

funny people

When you were at school, the funniest kid in the class was always a real pain in the neck. Liked by everyone, able to get away with more, they were someone to be 'in' with, whether you liked them or not. All those funny kids, where are they now? What happened to them, eh?

Well, some of them, annoyingly, became very rich and even more popular, their faces beamed into homes across the world. Fan clubs were set up to discuss nothing but these comedy heroes, articles were written about them and now whole sites of the internet have been given over to celebrating their successes. Well, what can you do?

These are just the tip of the comedy iceberg, but they are some of the best shrines dedicated to some of our funniest people. Love 'em or hate 'em, you can't ignore 'em. And, rest easy, chances are none of these went to your school anyway.

comedy

overall rating: ★ ★ ★ ★ ★	
classification: fan site	
updated: occasionally	
navigation: ★ ★ ★ ★ ★	
content: ★ ★ ★ ★	
readability: ★ ★ ★ ★ ★	
speed: ★ ★ ★ ★	
UK	

http://www.boyakasha.co.uk/index1.html
Boyakasha.co.uk

Ali G is one of the biggest comedy sensations for years. And, of course, there are loads of dedicated sites popping up all over the place. This is one of the best, combining all the best elements of its rivals. There's loads of information, pictures, news and other stuff. To give it an authentic ring, everything is written in the Ali G style of talking; if you're not a fan, it might become a little irritating after a while.

All the most recent news and information runs down the centre of the Homie page, but the real navigation is down the left-hand side in blue. The pages load fairly quickly and the content is good but updated infrequently.

SPECIAL FEATURES
Ali Info This is where you'll find all the funny background you need on Ali, from where he hangs out, to details of his friends and enemies. It's everything you need to know to be one of his massive (large gang – check out the Ali Dictionary for any words you're unsure of). At the bottom of the page you'll find some real information about the man behind the character, Sacha Baron Cohen.

Ali G Show A breakdown of the first Ali G series, section by section. There's information about who was on the show, along with some of the best lines from it.

Dictionary It may be embarrassing to admit that Ali G uses the odd word you don't fully understand, but help is at hand with this easy-to-use dictionary. Some of the language covered here might be unsuitable for children.

OTHER FEATURES

News Get all the latest on Ali G, but not updated very often.

Gallery A few dozen photos that are, on the whole, far too small and not of very high quality.

Sounds A variety of sounds from the Ali G show, including some of his best known phrases. There are also some much longer mp3s of Ali's brilliant interviews from the series, which are all worth revisiting.

Big Ups Want to say hi to someone? Want to converse in nothing but Ali G speak? Quite a lot of people leave messages but they are all very much in the same vein and occasionally vent a touch too much pent-up aggression.

An excellent site for all things Ali G, but only if you've seen his show. Otherwise it may be rather confusing.

comedy

overall rating: ★ ★ ★ ★ ★	
classification: guide	
updated: frequently	
navigation: ★ ★ ★ ★	
content: ★ ★ ★ ★ ★	
readability: ★ ★ ★ ★ ★	
speed: ★ ★ ★ ★ ★	
UK	

http://www.comedyonline.co.uk
Comedy Online

There's loads of live comedy up and down the country, and Comedy Online is one of the best ways to stay in touch with what's going on. It's a very detailed site, updated weekly, covering everything to do with the stand-up comedy circuit in the UK. It's bright, colourful, informative and the pages come thick and fast to your browser. Very slick. It's also an independent site, so you can be sure of an honest opinion. From the wildly yellow front page – click Do Come In to get to the meat of the site. Once inside you're faced with a message board type of page, with snippets of the latest news and stories, and links to other sites and what's currently going on. If you want an overview, click on the red links on the left.

SPECIAL FEATURES

News Lots of information about the comedians and the clubs they perform in. Find out who's going out on tour and where you can see them. Well-written snippets have links to the full story if you want more details. If you want to keep up to date, this should be your first stop.

Listings Firstly, decide if you want comedy in London or in the rest of the UK. Then click the relevant map. Follow the links to what you're looking for. A very useful resource in the London listings is the option to choose a date from the calendar and get all the live comedy in a single list, so you can plan your comedy night out much more easily. And if you want information even quicker, sign up for the newsletter.

Clubs If only all listings on the internet were this good. Choose from two maps, either of London or the whole of the UK. A single click brings up a comprehensive list of all the comedy venues in that area. You'll be amazed at how many clubs exist that you've never even heard of. All the addresses are there, as are all the phone numbers and even the nearest tube stations. Some venues have links to their own websites.

Become a Member If you're in the mood for filling in forms and you want to be sent more detailed information on 'upcoming events, special offers and inside juicy gossip', then why not become a member? A couple of minutes typing, nothing to pay, what have you got to lose?

Comedy Talk 'Chat Room' is a little misleading; actually, this is a bulletin board, but everyone posts in a very chatty manner so the discussions are easy to get into. It's not the busiest notice board on the internet, but a core of dedicated stand-up fans get involved in most of the discussion threads. So, if you have a question, you'll probably get a fairly informed reply.

Features Have you got a more detailed comment about comedy? Write it down, and if it's any good it might be featured on the site. The articles are not highbrow and are just the right length for a quick read. Be warned, though; other readers are invited to write articles in response to your own. If your thoughts are used, it's a much more rewarding way to have your say than posting in the Comedy Talk section.

Reviews Find out what the gigs you missed were like. The reviews are fairly short but well written and quite entertaining in themselves. The tone makes you feel like you're chatting to a mate about a gig he's just come back from.

OTHER FEATURES

Comedy Links Some great links to official and fan sites for some of the UK's best comedy performers, and some lesser known ones too.

Free Tickets A very useful little page. Find out what shows are soon to be recorded for television and how you can get free tickets to be part of the audience.

The whole site is great to look at, fast to download and well written. Its tone is friendly so you don't feel like you've stumbled on some exclusive site for hardened comedy-clubbers. If you've ever shown even the slightest interest in British stand-up comedy, then this is the place for you.

http://www.alan-partridge.co.uk
Dedicated Alan Partridge Site

Some people watched Knowing Me Knowing You with Alan Partridge and really had no idea what was going on. Others memorised every line and have made his humour part of their day-to-day banter. So, an acquired taste apparently, but if you ask us, he's one of the most original characters we've ever seen. As soon as you load up the first page of this website, you're reminded of just how funny he is. While the Partridge face jumps about the screen, click the coloured circles to hear classic Alan quips. When you've heard enough, click the button on the right to enter the site proper. You'll see from the front page that there are always several new bits of news every month, so it's easy to keep up with what's going on with the man from Norwich. The main links are on the left of this What's New page and appear on all the pages.

overall rating:
★ ★ ★ ★ ★

classification:
fan site

updated:
frequently

navigation:
★ ★ ★ ★ ★

content:
★ ★ ★ ★

readability:
★ ★ ★ ★ ★

speed:
★ ★ ★ ★ ★

UK

SPECIAL FEATURES

Video Clips Over 50 of Alan's most memorable moments from his shows. There's a little photo to remind you of what the clip's about, and if you click this it starts to download. The size of each clip is also mentioned, which is useful as, obviously, the bigger the clip, the longer the download time.

Sound Clips Loads of brilliant clips from the series, from one-liners to whole scenes. Every one of them a gem.

Scripts All six episodes from the I'm Alan Partridge series and two episodes from the radio show, transcribed at great length for your reading pleasure.

Message Board A fairly busy board, with almost exclusive Partridge content. It's easy to use and has a nice, fun feel to it. You do have to open an account with the board providers, but this is simple to do and free.

Guest Book Used a little like a secondary message board, which is a pain. But if you have something to say, or comment on, you can do it here without having to register and log on.

OTHER FEATURES

Pictures A smallish collection of photos, video captures and video box covers you can download or even set as wallpaper.

Links Lots of links to other Alan Partridge and Steve Coogan sites. Useful if you can't find what you're looking for here.

Screen Saver Fancy Alan's head bouncing around your screen to music? Of course you do. Download it here.

A nice and attractive site, with a user-friendly feel.

http://www.hancockontheweb.org.uk
Hancock on the Web

Although he died over 30 years ago, in 1968, a devout group of fans still herald Tony Hancock as the funniest comedian Britain has ever seen. From the opening page, you get the feeling that this is a genuinely heartfelt tribute site to someone who is sadly missed. Its grey background helps give the site a similar feel to the black and white series, Hancock's Half Hour. Some might say that it's a little drab, but this site is more about content than presentation, so you'll have to try and ignore its slightly old-fashioned style and typefaces. From the first page, click on the pictures of Hancock to get to the menu page. The links to move around are at the bottom of this page, and as the site is updated fairly regularly, it's worth remembering to check back now and then, especially as the episode guide is promised soon.

SPECIAL FEATURES

News Keep in touch with news about programmes, recordings and meetings. There are fairly frequent updates, but the old news isn't removed, so if you scroll down the page, don't make the mistake of applying for tickets for conventions that happened last year.

Reviews Informative reviews of books, recordings, videos and Hancock-related events, so you can stay up to date with what's available and whether it's worth investing in. Not exhaustive, but more reviews are promised.

overall rating:
★ ★ ★ ★ ★

classification:
fan site

updated:
regularly

navigation:
★ ★ ★ ★ ★

content:
★ ★ ★ ★ ★

readability:
★ ★ ★ ★

speed:
★ ★ ★ ★ ★

UK

Articles A collection of news reports and articles not only concerning Hancock, but also the writers and other actors who were involved in Hancock's Half Hour. Interesting and difficult to come by, these articles are a fascinating read.

Message Board If there's anything you want to know about Hancock or his work, there are some die-hard fans here who might be able to help. It's a fairly busy message board and most postings get at least one reply.

THAS Details of the Tony Hancock Appreciation Society and how to join.

OTHER FEATURES

Quiz Test your Hancockian knowledge with this 15-question quiz. If you're not at least a fairly avid fan, then forget it, try guessing.

Biographies Not only of Hancock, but also Kenneth Williams, Bill Kerr, Sid James, John Le Mesurier and Hattie Jacques, who all worked with him. Details of more co-stars are promised soon.

FAQ These are not questions at all, but rather some interesting snippets of Hancock trivia.

A very informative site, but not necessarily with mass appeal.

http://www.geocities.com/knipymarx/RandM.html
Mount McTwatty Bollocks
(The World of Reeves and Mortimer)

Love them or hate them, Vic and Bob are everywhere these days. If you've been wandering around the internet trying to find a site that lives up to the standard you expect with these two, you'll have been very disappointed. Most sites are sub-standard. But fear not, this is the ultimate in Reeves and Mortimer. It's up to date, loaded with information and other stuff, and it's the only Vic and Bob place worth going. The front page has up-to-the-minute news and is updated about once a week. To navigate, click the links under the green 'Contents' heading; be patient, as the pages are a little bit sluggish. Also, as it's a geocities site, you have to put up with their small pop-up windows appearing from time to time.

SPECIAL FEATURES

Productions A fantastic collection of information about everything Vic and Bob have ever done. Get details of their television work, books, videos, music, radio and even adverts.

Pictures Over 100 pictures arranged into various categories according to show, with sections for Vic and Bob, as individuals, further down the page. Unfortunately, a lot of the pictures are scanned from magazines, which means the quality is not great.

overall rating:	★ ★ ★ ★ ★
classification:	fan site
updated:	weekly
navigation:	★ ★ ★ ★ ★
content:	★ ★ ★ ★ ★
readability:	★ ★ ★ ★ ★
speed:	★ ★ ★ ★
UK	

Vic and Bob Fanclub For only £2, you can join the only fan club dedicated to Reeves and Mortimer. Some background and details of how to join by post are available here.

That Was A Good Joke Wasn't It? Some excellent and unusual features that wouldn't fit anywhere else. Enjoy a great series of cartoons depicting a week in the lives of Vic and Bob. Marvel at some of Vic Reeves' very own drawings of famous people. Then there's a really funny R and M product catalogue which consists of fictional items you can't actually buy.

Merchandise A pretty comprehensive list of Reeves and Mortimer things that can be bought on the web, with some links to where you can buy them. The prices are not necessarily guaranteed, so some shopping around is advised.

OTHER FEATURES

News This is a continuation of the news on the opening page. It has the added advantage of having monthly news archives.

Chat A link to a Reeves and Mortimer chat page on another site. Don't worry if there's no one there, join the scheduled chat every Sunday evening.

Interviews Loads of full-length interviews from the press.

Yahoo! Club Leave messages or chat with other fans online. Seems to be quite a teenage club.

Quite simply the only place worth bothering with if you want Reeves and Mortimer stimulation.

http://www.orangeneko.com/rik
Rik Mayall

Comedy wouldn't be where it is today without the arrival of 'alternative comedy', and Rik Mayall played a big part in that movement with Kevin Turvey, The Young Ones and The Comicstrip Presents. The simple style and easy navigation make this a wonderful place for finding out everything there is to know about one of our best-known television comedy actors. The links run down the right-hand side of his front page photo. Be warned; this incredibly in-depth site is put together by someone with devotion way beyond the call of duty, and you may lose several months experiencing it. Not only that, but it looks quite pleasant and the pages load quickly. It's updated at least once a week, often more frequently, and you can sign up for an e-mail informing you when there's something new. You get the feeling you've stepped into a living and breathing Rik Mayall fan community. Can't really fault it.

SPECIAL FEATURES

News Very informative and updated two or three times a month, or whenever there's something to report. There's information about forthcoming television programmes, articles and even mention of new adverts Rik has lent his voice to.

Biography Brief information about his beginnings and major turning points in his career.

overall rating:	★ ★ ★ ★ ★
classification:	fan site
updated:	frequently
navigation:	★ ★ ★ ★ ★
content:	★ ★ ★ ★ ★
readability:	★ ★ ★ ★ ★
speed:	★ ★ ★ ★ ★

UK

His Projects If you thought Rik Mayall was responsible for little more than some daft, face-pulling characters who offend your Grandmother, then this enormous list should put you straight. He doesn't seem old enough to have done so much work.

Photos No fan site is complete without its photo collection and this site has literally hundreds. As well as publicity shots there are also lots of screen grabs from television appearances. A brilliant photo collection.

The Rik Library Nearly 100 complete interviews and articles from every conceivable publication.

By the Fans Feel the need to write something of your own? A review, a poem, or even a story? You can send your scribblings in here, and they might even end up on the site for everyone to see. Currently, there are some enormous fan fictions and some depressingly devoted fan poems. Not for the faint-hearted.

Discussion Board Fairly busy boards where, thankfully, most postings are to the point and about Rik-related things.

OTHER FEATURES

TV Listings An incomplete list of where Rik can be seen on the box in Britain, America, Australia and the Rest of the World.

Quotes Split into manageable sections of his career, this is a huge list of quotes from interviews rather than funny catch phrases and jokes.

Screensavers and Wavs Consists of six screensavers and two large wavs for Living Doll and All the Little Flowers are Happy.

Where to Buy Rik Items A huge list of places that sell items relating to Rik and his work. If you can't find what you want from one of these places, you must have imagined the thing you want and it doesn't exist.

If only all fan sites were even half as detailed and informative as this one. Quite simply, excellent.

comedy

overall rating: ★ ★ ★ ★ ★	
classification: ezine	
updated: frequently	
navigation: ★ ★ ★ ★ ★	
content: ★ ★ ★ ★ ★	
readability: ★ ★ ★ ★ ★	
speed: ★ ★ ★ ★ ★	
UK	

http://www.users.dircon.co.uk/~wilco
Standupcom.com Magazine

Many of the funniest people in the country are the unsung heroes of the stand-up comedy circuit, facing the heckles of the crowd until that big break comes and they become a team captain on a celebrity panel show. This monthly ezine is about them, and it is filled with 'reviews, interviews and comedy gossip'. It's written in a very intelligent, friendly way but doesn't avoid honest opinions, whether they're complimentary or scathing. The site itself has an old-fashioned feel, wasting no time on fancy graphics, pointless sections to pad out the site or multimedia clutter. It relies on up-to-the-minute content, interesting articles and honest-to-goodness quality writing. The links to get around are under the main title and are available on every subsequent page too.

SPECIAL FEATURES

News and Gossip Snippets of news from the comedy grapevine. A small, intimate section of the site, with more or less content depending on what's going on in the world of stand-up comedy.

Reviews Lots of excellent reviews of live comedy in the last few weeks. Although it promises to cover stand-up all over Britain, the emphasis is definitely on London clubs. The reviews have a friendly, honest tone, which helps you get a feel for all the comedians mentioned. You could easily make an informed choice on who you would like to see at a later date from these reviews, and even which comedy clubs you might fancy popping into. Most of the reviews capture the atmosphere of the night in question, and they will have you yearning to get back into the comedy scene and enjoy these comics first-hand. If you're looking for something from the past, there is a link to the archives at the bottom of the page.

Interviews A small but growing collection of interviews with some of the best comedians around, including Alan Davies and Phill Jupitus, twice.

Comedy Shop As well as running this site, Standupcom also runs a London comedy club that takes place once a month. You can book very reasonable tickets here or even book a whole event for your special occasion.

Well written and to the point. An excellent stand-up comedy site.

comedy

overall rating: ★ ★ ★ ★ ★
classification: official site
updated: regularly
navigation: ★ ★ ★ ★ ★
content: ★ ★ ★ ★ ★
readability: ★ ★ ★ ★ ★
speed: ★ ★ ★ ★ ★
UK

http://www.izzard.com
The Official Eddie Izzard Website

Possibly the funniest man alive on the planet today. And his official website's not bad either. He's not everyone's cup of tea, especially as he looks good in women's clothes and his humour is brilliantly off-the-wall. But if you're here, you've obviously got an interest, so click Eddie's face to get into the site and don't be misled by the suggestion that there are only three parts to the site; there are four. Once inside, the four links are on the left. You can either click the name of the section or follow the yellow arrow and click where it points. Either way you end up in the same place, at a selection of sub-headings which take you to more specific details. At the bottom of the page you'll find the same four links again, so navigation couldn't be simpler. Everything appears between the two blue curtains and has great style. The site doesn't keep to the same format for every section, so there are lots of surprise bits, like photos, sounds and information you didn't know you were going to get. The news and information sections are updated as and when there's something new to say. And what makes this site the best Izzard site is that it's the one Eddie himself occasionally posts to and gets involved with.

SPECIAL FEATURES

Comedy Stage A short but informative piece on each of his major comedy stand-up shows. Some just receive a brief outline, some have more detailed information and even some snippets of his material, and Lenny contains rehearsal and performance photos, press quotes and even audio clips. Take a wander through this section and you'll be pretty well versed in the career of Eddie Izzard. And, if you're interested, you can read the same pages in French.

Centre Stage There's some background reading on Eddie, by Eddie, along with all the latest news and even his horoscope. If you're in the mood to expand your Izzard video collection, there's information about what's available; sadly, you can't buy directly from here. However, there is a link to the Official Merchandise site, which is very impressively designed and has loads of stuff you can buy securely online. If you're in the mood for some silliness, there are also a couple of screensavers which you can download, as well as a sheep who will wander around your desktop. Most importantly, keep an eye on Tour Dates. If Eddie's going to be live near you, this is where you're likely to read it first.

Film Stage Details of films he's appeared in. Oddly, the emphasis is on briefly reviewing the film, rather than saying anything about Eddie's roles or performances. Still, that's the difference between 'official' and 'fan' sites, which sometimes can't see anything but their never-ending devotion to their hero.

Eddie's World There's a fairly active message board, frequented by a devoted group who practically use the board as a chat room. There's a lot being posted that has nothing to do with Eddie. The Square Window contains a disappointingly small collection of photos, but more are promised. There's Eddie's World, which is two mailing lists, one of which contains occasional postings from the man himself. There's also a great idea of helping to write a book online, but it's all a bit messy and not terribly user-friendly.

A great site which is more intelligent and less slavering with adoration than a lot of celebrity sites.

http://www.btinternet.com/~sarsen/billy/billy.html
Billy Connolly

It claims to be the first Billy Connolly Web site and it may very well be, but at the moment it's going through a period of change, with major updates imminent. Don't let that put you off though, because there's still plenty of useful content. As a fan, you may already own some of the videos and recordings, but you'll be surprised at how many others there are to buy. The complete listings are very useful for checking on your collection and keeping it up to date. When you've found a recording you want, it would be great if you could follow a link to an online shop that's selling it. But you can't. You have to make a note of the title and find it yourself at the shop of your choice. Navigate using the links at the very top of the front page, which are available from any part of the site. You'll quickly notice that, for such a funny comedian, the web design is a little too dull and, well, green.

overall rating:	★ ★ ★ ★
classification:	fan site
updated:	infrequently
navigation:	★ ★ ★ ★ ★
content:	★ ★ ★
readability:	★ ★ ★ ★
speed:	★ ★ ★ ★ ★
UK	

SPECIAL FEATURES

Biography An excellent, very detailed account of Billy's life, from his early days right up to the present. The story is told with great love and affection and is peppered with lots of photos.

Jokes If your browser can cope with Java script, you'll see a brilliant selection of Billy's jokes and quips scroll across the screen. You can control the speed using the Slower and Faster buttons. If you'd prefer, the jokes are also available in plain text, just follow the link. These jokes are exactly as Billy would have performed them, swearing and all.

OTHER FEATURES

Videos A list, with photos, of every Billy Connolly live performance video.

Records Most of the recordings also feature a photo of the album cover; none of the reviews are complete, but they are promised soon.

Books An archive of all the available Billy Connolly books, with brief reviews and an invitation to contact the site if you know of any that are missing.

Movies A complete list of Billy's movies is still in the process of being constructed. It promises to give details of the director and the supporting actors, but not at the moment.

Sounds Some funny sound clips from Billy's stand up shows. They're all pretty short, so you don't have to worry too much about download times.

Photos A disappointingly small collection of photos for a fan site, but all the thumbnails are clickable to get a larger picture.

FAQ This is painfully incomplete, but once again, more is promised in the near future.

A very well-organised site from a devoted fan. Will be even better if it's ever fully complete.

http://members.aol.com/damsel16/sellers1.html
Darla's Peter Sellers Tribute Page

Hard to believe that Sellers died over 20 years ago, and in case you can't quite remember the name of the series of films for which he's best known, the Pink Panther theme plays over and over as you read his biography and some interesting trivia on the front page. Just below the 'Did You Know's are the main links for the site. A lot of the pages are rather academic in tone, most giving interesting but not terribly inspiring lists of basic information. However, Darla promises that a major revamp is on the way, with both improved content and design.

SPECIAL FEATURES

Filmography This page lists all of Sellers' films and short films. Most have a rating of one to four stars, and a handful have links to full page reviews.

Being There Not a terribly busy notice board, but there are always a core of fans willing to try and answer questions, or at least point you in the right direction. Postings rarely stray from the subject of Sellers and there's no need to register, so just read some posts then have your say.

Java Slide Show A great idea but could be made much longer. A handful of photos appear in a slideshow while Darla tells you a little about them.

overall rating:
★ ★ ★ ★

classification:
fan site

updated:
occasionally

navigation:
★ ★ ★ ★ ★

content:
★ ★ ★

readability:
★ ★ ★ ★

speed:
★ ★ ★ ★ ★

US

OTHER FEATURES

Discography   A huge list of Sellers recordings. Enormously tempting to any collector or fan, but frustratingly there's no information about what is still available, what has been re-issued onto CD, or where the best place is to buy any of it.

Television   Only for the Sellers addict, a long list of his TV appearances both here and in America. It's not complete, nor is it filled with shows that most will have heard of.

Sellers TV Now Listings   You'll be surprised just how many of Peter Sellers' films are being shown on the television in any given month. Unfortunately, the listings are all for American TV.

A nice but basic site which could benefit from an expansion which, hopefully, is on the way.

http://www.geocities.com/Broadway/Wing/7381/index.html
Draylon Underground's Harmonising Homepage

Just to prove that you don't have to be wildly famous – with your own television show and guest spots on celebrity panel shows – to be funny, here's something unusual: Close Harmony Comedy. However, they're not a new outfit. They've been around for more than 14 years, have been regulars at the Comedy Store and have appeared on various radio and television shows. They attack all kinds of musical styles with rich satire and humour, and should be more famous than they actually are.

Don't be put off by the fact that the page counter says you're visitor number 0000, it must be broken. It's very easy to get around the site; just click on the black and maroon boxes on the left. It's not currently updated, but if you like the sound of them, check out http:\\www.mp3.com\draylonunderground, which is their MP3.com page.

SPECIAL FEATURES

About Us If this is your first experience of Close Harmony Comedy, you can get some background on the group here.

Hear Us Download a brilliantly original and satirical song. Guaranteed to bring a smile to your face, if not have you laughing out loud.

overall rating:	★★★★
classification:	homepage
updated:	not
navigation:	★★★★★
content:	★★★
readability:	★★★★★
speed:	★★★★
UK	

comedy

See Us Strangely, this section is either not kept fully up to date, or the group have had trouble getting gigs. You can always email them and demand more information. They are also very keen to be hired to perform at venues of your choosing. They'll even custom build their set to your preferences and possibly write some original songs for you. Obviously it will be at a price, but they'd be a fantastic addition to any event you were planning. Contact them for more details.

Worth the visit for the downloadable song alone, but the site could do with more content, updates and songs.

http://www.frenchandsaunders.com
French and Saunders

This lively website, celebrating Britain's most successful female double act, is heaven for those who like meandering around a site, browsing at random. At times it seems that there is no part of any page which is not clickable. Links are everywhere, to the point that if you're not careful you could end up going round in circles. The content is clear, fairly informative and up-to-the-minute. From the front page, your first choice is between one of the grey boxes on the right or the news running down the page. Click a headline to go to the full story, or follow the link called More News for, you guessed it, more news. The site is a little on the plain side and the content is more informative than fun; but for an overview of French and Saunders, it's great.

SPECIAL FEATURES

News Snippets of information about Dawn and Jennifer and what they've been up to. It would be nice if there was more exclusive news, as most of the short- to medium-length articles present information that is available in the press. However, to have it all in the one place is a definite bonus.

Shows Reviews of the various shows French and Saunders are involved with, including their Christmas Specials and Jennifer Saunders' new comedy Mirrorball, which is expected in the not too distant future.

overall rating:	★ ★ ★ ★
classification:	official site
updated:	occasionally
navigation:	★ ★ ★ ★
content:	★ ★ ★ ★
readability:	★ ★ ★ ★ ★
speed:	★ ★ ★
UK	

comedy

Faces French and Saunders are well known for their hilarious parodies of films and musical videos, but just in case you've forgotten a couple of these 'unforgettable' comedy moments, here's an A to Z list linking to photos and summaries.

Cast Too brief summaries of French and Saunders, Joanna Lumley, Julia Sawalha and Jane Horrocks. Guest Stars is a rather misleading heading; it turns out to be little more than a couple of paragraphs listing celebrities who have appeared on French and Saunders.

Crew Biographies of Richard Curtis (writer), Jon Plowman (producer) and Bob Spiers (director). All of them have worked extensively with French and Saunders.

Discussion Forums Six fairly active message boards, organised into discussions relevant to different French and Saunders productions. You need to register before you can post a message, but it's fairly quick to do and completely free. There are currently about 150 registered members.

The site would benefit from some expanding and lacks certain 'fan' elements such as photo collections, sounds and anything interactive. However, it's a good dip-in site for fans who want an overview.

http://www.users.globalnet.co.uk/~hkev
Paul Merton Unofficial

Perhaps best known for Have I Got News For You, Paul Merton is one of Britain's most recognisable comedians. The site is very busy and there's lots to see and read. The full navigation links are down the left of the front page, but there are abbreviated links on the other pages, which doesn't look great but saves you having to click the back button to get around. There's not much organisational thought gone into the site but the content makes up for that, and who says organisation is good? There's an interesting mix of fact and comedy, funny and hit-and-miss, but there's plenty to browse around. Updated about once a month.

overall rating:	★★★★
classification:	fan site
updated:	monthly
navigation:	★★★★★
content:	★★★★
readability:	★★★★
speed:	★★★★★
UK	

SPECIAL FEATURES

The Life of Merton A detailed, chronological list of his work.

Missing Words If you are a fan of Merton on Have I Got News for You, you might recognise some of these hilarious replies he made during the Missing Word round.

History of the 20th Century A fairly amusing extract from Merton's book of the same title.

Author Author! Interesting background on Merton the scriptwriter.

Policeman in Court A brilliant script to one of Merton's early monologues.

My Struggle Excerpts from his fictional autobiography.

OTHER FEATURES

Merton For Sale Videos, books, recordings and details of where some of them can be bought online.

Merton's Mistakes Some fairly funny fictional career choice mistakes.

Merton and 'Friends' Never having held back when talking about his feelings for people, here is a collection of some of the funniest and rudest comments he has made about some very high-profile people.

News Infrequent snippets about Merton's television and radio appearances.

Virtual News Quiz Clever idea, but the random appearance of quips from Merton, Angus Deayton and Ian Hislop doesn't really work in practice.

An interesting mix of fact and frivolity.

http://www.geocities.com/CollegePark/7136/gindex.htm
The Information SuperGoonway

A newish site dedicated to that hilarious British Comedy phenomenon, The Goons. If you're not a fan and are unfamiliar with some of the characters, a little of the site's content might be bewildering, as it's written in the tone of voice of the character speaking. But you'll soon get used to it, as the site is extremely helpful and friendly. Get around by using the links on the right. It's unclear how often the site gets updated. If you're still not satisfied, or want a site that concentrates on the actual performers a bit more, you might want to take a look at The Goon Show Preservation Society at http://www.goonshow.org.uk/index.htm.

SPECIAL FEATURES

Introduction Just in case you didn't get the sound clip when you opened the page, click here for a suitably big-band introduction that sets the tone and style for the rest of the site. Go on, it's got a built-in feel-good factor.

Henry Crun's History of the Goons Slightly too brief for those uneducated in the world of the Goons, but as far as it goes, it's informative and easy to read.

Miss Minnie Bannister's Character References Do you think Eccles is a cake and Bluebottle a big nasty fly? You need to have a look at this list of characters and read up on their particulars.

overall rating:	★ ★ ★ ★
classification:	fan site
updated:	occasionally
navigation:	★ ★ ★ ★ ★
content:	★ ★ ★ ★
readability:	★ ★ ★
speed:	★ ★ ★ ★ ★
UK	

You can also download a ludicrously short clip of the character speaking. This page informs you that each character here has a colour reference. If you see writing in that colour elsewhere on the site, it indicates that the person is speaking. That might have been a useful note for the front page.

Grytpype-Thynne's Script Stop Eighteen complete scripts for you to download or read online.

A useful place to introduce yourself to the show and its characters, but like a lot of fan sites dedicated to old shows, updates are fairly infrequent.

http://www.morecambeandwise.co.uk
The Morecambe and Wise Homepage

Probably the best loved British comedy duo of all time. It's a shame that there isn't a more comprehensive collection of career details and trivia, but what there is, is well presented and the site, if a little basic, is quick and smooth. The links to navigate the site run down the left-hand side, and a selection of these are available from each and every page, not just the front one. 'Major Revisions' are promised soon.

SPECIAL FEATURES

Shop Without a doubt, the best section of the site. Not only is there a fairly comprehensive list of recordings and videos, but there are direct links to where they can be bought.

Biographies For comedians whose careers spanned so many decades, their biographies are terribly thin. However, it is interesting to read how the two came to meet.

TV and Radio A very interesting list of Eric and Ernie's performances, firstly on the radio, then on TV.

Mailing List If you want to stay in touch with other fans of Morecambe and Wise, why not sign up for the free list? You can choose whether to have individual posts or daily mailings. If you do sign up for the list, you also get access to a Morecambe and Wise chat room. Sadly, though, there's very often no one else there.

overall rating:	★ ★ ★ ★
classification:	fan site
updated:	occasionally
navigation:	★ ★ ★ ★ ★
content:	★ ★ ★
readability:	★ ★ ★ ★
speed:	★ ★ ★ ★ ★
UK	

Screen Saver There's only one screen saver available at the moment, but more are promised in the near future. It's worth downloading and is quite touching as Eric and Ernie sing Bring Me Sunshine.

OTHER FEATURES

Some rather outdated news, a too-small collection of photos and a noticeboard with surprisingly little traffic.

Overall the content is on the thin side, but what's there is pretty good. Morecambe and Wise really deserve a more comprehensive site, but this is definitely the best out there so far.

OTHER SITES OF INTEREST

RadioHaHa

http://www.angelfire.com/pq/radiohaha/asdf.html

It's easy to forget just how much comedy programming goes out on the radio, but this site certainly sets the record straight. It's not an attractive site to look at, but if you want to know anything about radio comedy during the 1980s and 1990s, this really has to be the place to come. Amongst other sections, there's a huge, alphabetical list of writers, producers and actors, a frequently asked questions page, and a huge list of programmes, each of which has a summary page when you click on their title.

timewasters

There are times in everybody's life when the thought of having to get on with whatever you have to get on with becomes the single hardest thing in the world to do. Everything becomes a distraction, an excuse to ignore life's priorities. Well, why struggle? Give in, relax, life's too short. And don't bother wasting time doing something mundane like de-fluffing your navel, really get into something funny but ultimately pointless, like one of these sites.

There are jokes and gags and a million things to bring a smile to your face. Everything needed to help the clock tick round to a time when it's too late to bother with whatever you should have been doing in the first place.

There really is something for everyone here. Unless you're a workaholic, in which case you'll be far too busy to even think about enjoying yourself, let alone read this guide.

http://pen-web.com/rainyday/alexwarp/alexwarp.htm
Alex Warp

Whether you're young or old, there are times when life gets too much, when the stresses and strains of work or home begin to take their toll. You know the feeling, the milkman left full fat, there's nowhere to park, your boss has dedicated his day to making your life a misery. Or maybe it's simply raining outside, it's cold and depressing and you want to start screaming at people. Don't take it out on your friends and family. Take it out on the rich and famous from the comfort of your own chair. Use Alex Warp to make your world a better place. And if not, this daft page should at least make you laugh.

It's so simple it's brilliant. Choose a face, any face. There are dozens of famous names to choose from. A new window appears with the photo of your choice. Click anywhere on or around the picture, drag the pointer in any direction and simply let go, and watch the face distort. Make Bruce Willis look like Bruce Forsyth, Keanu Reeves like Vic Reeves, and Mariah Carey more like Jim Carrey.

It's fun, strangely addictive and more socially acceptable than running out into the street screaming. The only downside is that it's American so you might not have heard of all the celebrities. It's updated periodically and you can influence how (see below).

overall rating:
★ ★ ★ ★ ★

classification:
homepage

updated:
regularly

navigation:
★ ★ ★ ★ ★

content:
★ ★ ★ ★

readability:
★ ★ ★ ★ ★

speed:
★ ★ ★ ★ ★

US

SPECIAL FEATURES

Pick a Face This is really the only feature on the site. There are a number of celebrities who are in line for the 'warp' treatment and you can vote to decide who's next. If your personal favourite isn't there, just fill in the box at the bottom of the page and your wish will be noted.

Pointless it may be, but there is no denying it's incredible fun to mess about with.

http://www.digitallaughter.com
Digital Laughter.com

One of the problems with sites that 'collect' funny material from around the net is that quantity often wins over quality. This site is a collection of some of the 'best' humour off the web, and it still boasts a substantial archive of stuff. So you get the best of both worlds. There is something for everyone here, but you may have to wade through some material you don't find funny before you get what you want. The only type of humour that gets singled out is Adult humour, which always has a warning. Everything else you take a chance on; but, as most things load pretty quickly, you'll soon find something to make you laugh. If you have something that you think is funny, you're more than welcome to send it to the site, and if they like it they'll include it. Updates are every couple of weeks, and navigation couldn't be simpler.

SPECIAL FEATURES

Funny Images From standard joke cartoons to much funnier real-life photos and professional stills, this is a great collection of humorous images. There are five sections to choose from, but the content is not in any particular order. After clicking on a title, the photos open individually on a new page. Just hit the Back button when you want another. There's even a page containing a thumbnail for every image. It takes a little while to load them all but it gives you a better idea of what you're getting.

overall rating:	★ ★ ★ ★ ★
classification:	homepage
updated:	fortnightly
navigation:	★ ★ ★ ★ ★
content:	★ ★ ★ ★ ★
readability:	★ ★ ★ ★
speed:	★ ★ ★ ★
US	

comedy

Funny Video Clips These clips, which obviously take longer to download, are sorted into categories according to content, which varies from home-movie slapstick to more unpleasant clips of people getting hurt.

Funny Downloads Proof that even small programmes can be funny. There are loads of really good downloads. Some of them are quite infantile and probably aimed at a slightly more male sense of humour, but everyone will find something they just love. You watch, you'll end up trying them all.

Web Funnies These are great interactive games and stuff. The games aren't funny but some of them are absolutely excellent as free downloads. Matix is especially good and worth a look.

OTHER FEATURES

Sound Clips These range from some great home-made clips to Comedians performing in their live shows.

Bill Clinton Funnies Probably funnier to those who had to be governed by him, but still an amusing collection of photos and cartoons, some of which are animated.

Mind Teasers Don't really belong on a comedy site, but are interesting if you're mathematically minded.

Daily Cartoons One pretty funny cartoon a day, and the option to get more if you want.

A great variety of comedy of a well-above average standard.

http://www.humournet.co.uk
Humour Net

Basically this site is just another collection of jokes and daft pictures. What makes it stand out, though, is that it is very well ordered and easy to get around. Navigation is simple; just click the links on the left, which open up pages with more specific choices. It's updated every week or two.

SPECIAL FEATURES

Jokes Now, jokes by themselves would not normally make it as a 'special feature'. However, if you click on Main Jokes Page you get such a big selection of categorised jokes, some familiar and some rather more unusual than the internet norm, that it simply has to be mentioned. For instance, you could actually use some of the funny Answerphone Messages on your own machine. The Court Room Quotations are great and give you faith in our justice system. Some of the insults are quite abusive, but you'll find yourself laughing. And so it goes on. Each section has a star rating so you can see what other visitors thought were the best jokes. You can add your vote at the bottom of each page.

Funny Pictures Dozens of very funny pictures, photos and cartoons. Some of them may offend and there's a warning to that effect at the top of each page.

Cool Downloads Some of these have been doing the rounds for some time, but some may be new to you. It is amazing to

overall rating:
★ ★ ★ ★ ★

classification:
homepage

updated:
weekly(ish)

navigation:
★ ★ ★ ★ ★

content:
★ ★ ★ ★ ★

readability:
★ ★ ★ ★

speed:
★ ★ ★ ★ ★

UK

think that this is what talented people do when they have some time on their hands. If you don't know where to start try Fart. You know it's infantile, you know you shouldn't be smirking, but you probably will be. An absolute must is the Desktop, which is not only great fun, but also a necessity when you're having a bad day.

Excellent site. Claims to be funny, and is.

http://www.heenan.net/trivia/index.html
Pi in the Sky

The most unusual thing about this site is that its owner is very keen that we should get more than just random gag after gag; instead, they're collected into jokes of the same type. Often we're given a little background on the joke and some pointers on how to properly create a new one. That said, most of the jokes are well written and pretty funny, and he's been very conscientious and rewritten some of the smuttier jokes so they're suitable for a wider audience. If you think you know any better jokes that belong in his collections, he's very happy for you to send them in. Pi in the Sky is a slick site, simple but not unattractively designed and very easy to navigate. You'll find the main links are next to the pieces of pie on the left of the front page. There's so much here to enjoy that it isn't terribly important that the site is only updated every few months.

SPECIAL FEATURES

W-W-Words Ever so slightly more highbrow than a lot of humour on the internet. This is a humorous dictionary with a variety of sources giving the definitions. These range from Ambrose Bierce's biting irony, cockney rhyming slang, invented words for things that don't have a name and quotes from famous people. A very interesting wander through the humour of our language.

Light Bulbs From Academics to Zen Masters, no type of person is ignored from the famous 'How many does it take to change a

overall rating:	★ ★ ★ ★ ★
classification:	homepage
updated:	occasionally
navigation:	★ ★ ★ ★ ★
content:	★ ★ ★ ★ ★
readability:	★ ★ ★ ★ ★
speed:	★ ★ ★ ★ ★
UK	

light bulb?'. As with all 'theme' jokes, some you will find quite funny (Mystery Writers) and some not funny (Historians). If you have been living on another planet and do not know how these jokes work, there is a section, About Light Bulb Jokes, which explains all. It even lists five notes that should be considered when inventing a new one. Possibly more information than we needed to know.

Genie Jokes An excellent collection of funnies, nearly all of which are suitable for family consumption. Once again, there is an introduction to this kind of joke and some interesting observations about them. If you're in a slightly more smutty frame of mind, try the Smutty Genie Jokes.

OTHER FEATURES

Some of these are hidden away within the site. Click on one of the above links and you'll get some more choices down the left of the page that opens up.

Tall Tales A pretty good collection of longer jokes. There's very little here that's unsuitable for an audience of any age.

Two Cows A couple of cows are used to explain a whole series of political ideologies. Clever but highbrow.

Microsoft Bill Gates and his empire come in for more scathing attacks. Only funny if you've experienced computer problems or know anything about the American billionaire.

Real Names A list of more than 2,000 famous people and their real names. When you read that English rose, Jane Seymour, was actually born 'Joyce Frankenberg', you can see why they changed them.

Tommy Cooper A collection of some of the great comedian's funniest jokes.

Johnny and Mary Excellent jokes about the most notable kids in the classroom.

A joke site that has actually had some time and effort spent on it is a rare thing, as are collections of jokes that are mostly funny. This is one such site, and it's a great place to start collecting good gags.

comedy

overall rating:	★ ★ ★ ★ ★
classification:	homepage
updated:	regularly
navigation:	★ ★ ★ ★ ★
content:	★ ★ ★ ★ ★
readability:	★ ★ ★ ★ ★
speed:	★ ★ ★ ★ ★

http://www.rinkworks.com
Rinkworks

Rinkworks is a huge site that has everything you might need to get you through a long, cold, rainy day. There are things to do, things to play, things to send and places to communicate with other people. There are also some really funny areas, guaranteed to put a smile back on your face. The Site Index runs down the left of the page in the blue box. If you want a little explanation of what you'll find beyond each link, try looking in the Site Guide first. The link for this is in the centre of the page, just under the heading New Readers. You'll find the funny bits under the main headings of Humour and Humour Bites. The site is updated regularly, so even if you have months of long, cold, rainy days, you'll always be able to find something new.

SPECIAL FEATURES

Things People Said One of the funniest parts of the site. What you get here is a collection of things that people have actually said. From accident reports to the crazy things children say, this will have you wondering how so many ridiculous people survive in the world today. The Accident Reports and The Courtroom Quotations have been doing the rounds for years, but if you haven't read them you must. They're the pick of the bunch.

Movie-a-Minute Love films? No time to watch them? Then this is the perfect place for you. Whole films summed up in under a minute. Some are very funny but after a while the joke starts to wear a bit thin. Also, to get the most out of them, you really have to have seen the full-length version. Book-a-Minute is, not unsurprisingly, the same joke applied to the written word.

Computer Stupidities A huge collection of real-life funnies about computers, their users and the problems they encounter. Most of them are reports of people phoning help lines and not having a clue what they're talking about, others are almost considered to be urban myths and have been circulating the internet for years. If you know anything about computers you'll find a lot of these funny. However, some of them are very technical and will mean little or nothing to those without real expertise.

Really Bad Jokes This doesn't need explanation. Care must be taken when reading these as they really are bad. Terrible. So bad they're funny.

Don't Throw a Brick Straight Up Some important instructions for us all. Some are obvious, such as 'Don't eat rocks'; some are ridiculous, such as 'Wash behind your ears, not your eyes'; and some are simply funny, like 'Don't brush your teeth with a wire-bristled sanding wheel'.

Pea Soup for the Cynic's Soul Some excellent and original stories that will rekindle in your heart the knowledge that happy endings have no place in the real world. Some real gems.

A good site for all-round entertainment, with an excellent variety of humour.

comedy

overall rating: ★★★★	
classification: homepage	
updated: occasionally	
navigation: ★★★★★	
content: ★★★★	
readability: ★★★★	
speed: ★★★	
UK	

http://www.beebfun.com
beebfun

You know what it's like, you spend so much time at your computer you get bored looking at the same old drab colours and pictures. Look no further. Beebfun has a large collection of comedy related desktop themes, from Porridge and The Fast Show to Wallace and Gromit and Auf Wiedersehen Pet. You get new pictures for the start up and shutting down windows, new wallpaper and icons, a new screensaver and even some new sounds to replace the usual boring beeps. They only work on Windows 95 and higher, but if you're still using Windows 3.1, it really is time for a serious upgrade. Navigation is done by clicking the links in the frame on the left. There's plenty to choose from already but every now and then they add something new, so keep your eyes peeled. The only downside, if you can call it one, is that all the desktop themes relate to the best of British comedy. If you're after something American, you'll have to look elsewhere.

SPECIAL FEATURES

Desktop Themes These are what you want. All the themes you can cope with. At the last count there were nearly 50, so don't download them all at once. All the pages have links to relevant sites, and you also get told how big the file you want to download is. Very useful; you can start a download and go and put the kettle on.

Theme Managers   Once you've got all these new downloads, you really need something to help you install and store them. Listed here are five free programmes you can download in only a few minutes. All these are excellent, and having one is an absolute must.

More TV Themes   These are links to even more British TV themes from other websites. Just if you need a change.

OTHER FEATURES

Theme Resources   Lots of links to other sites where desktop themes can be found.

Comedy Links   If you want some more information about some of the television programmes you've seen here, try checking this fairly comprehensive list of sites.

If you want to change the way your computer looks, you need a good choice of themes to pick from. This is an easy site for getting just what you want, and quickly.

comedy

http://www.comedycircus.com/home_js.html
Comedy Circus.com

You could spend several days roaming around this mammoth site, which is a fairly good place to start if you're putting off something far more important. The beauty of the Comedy Circus is that it includes a bit of anything you could want from the world of comedy. It's got a funky design, but the link descriptions don't necessarily make navigation as simple as it might be. But who said comedy should be simple? You can read stuff, play games, get involved, and even buy videos and recordings. The light purple links in the centre of the page take you to the different parts of the site. If you're looking for something more specific, some sub-headings appear to get you there quicker. When you're finished with a section, and you're viewing the site with frames, you don't even have to hop back to the homepage, all those links can be found beneath the six symbols on the left of each page.

Although it's nice to look at and great fun to wander around, the pages do have a habit of taking an age to load and reload.

SPECIAL FEATURES

Meet Me Get the low down on the best of British Comedians. There are biographies on a few of the up-and-coming comedy acts, as well as already established stand-ups including Joe Brand, Ben Elton and Frankie Howard. Oddly, these are in alphabetical order according to their first names rather than their surnames. For each comedian you can listen to previews of their act and then buy their CD if you like what you hear. There's also a less than complete roundup of live comedy around the country.

Buy Me Buy a variety of comedy items, including Videos, CDs and MP3s. You have to register first before buying. All payments online are secure, so you can purchase with confidence.

Play Me Download flash games and cartoons, including some bizarre re-enactments of famous scenes from films with Jelly Babies as the characters and the groan-worthy Stand Up Dog, who retells some of the world's oldest gags. There's also comedy poetry, some excellent ecards made with cartoons, and cut-outs of famous people's faces. There are even a few desktop wallpapers and screen savers to download.

Humour Me This is the place for you to get involved, complete quizzes or submit your own hysterical entry in the caption competition. Soon you'll be able to send in your own funny videos, animations, images and audio files for everyone to enjoy.

Hear Me The free MP3 clips, in one place for easy downloading.

Read Me If you register you can have the site's weekly email magazine sent to you for free. There are some back issues you can read online. You get a great mixture of funny, made-up news stories, jokes and various jokes from famous comedians. Worth a look.

A bit of everything without swamping you with loads of inappropriate rubbish. An easy place to waste some time.

comedy

overall rating:	★ ★ ★ ★
classification:	homepage
updated:	frequently
navigation:	★ ★ ★ ★
content:	★ ★ ★
readability:	★ ★ ★ ★
speed:	★ ★ ★

 UK **18**

http://www.pykersjokes.com/topsites/index.html
Naughty Humour

Every now and then, you fancy something a little bit stronger, be it your coffee in the morning, or your daily tipple. The same is true with comedy. Many people find 'adult' humour offensive, and if you're one of them you should stay away from this site. For the rest of us there's plenty to laugh at here and apparently it's updated every 30 minutes. There's loads of bad language and adult-only subject matter in these pages, but if you're not easily offended, you'll be laughing. The links in this site are the four boxes directly under the front page. The rest are links to other adult comedy sites. Be warned: if you start browsing these other links, as well as the sites you clicked on, there are often random windows opening trying to get you to go somewhere else. If you're not careful, after a few minutes of clicking around you can have dozens of open windows and be completely lost. Basically, if you click a link and another window opens while you're waiting for the page to load, simply close it straight away.

SPECIAL FEATURES

Funny Videos The content is quite varied, including expressions of anger, some nudity, and some barefaced silliness. They take a while to download, as always.

Naughty Jokes You can read random jokes and jokes by subject.

Don't think you can avoid the adult content by not clicking on the Sex and Crude subject headings, everything contains something that would make you blush in front of your mother.

Adult Pics Click on the individual pics from the last few days or click the Archive button for something with a title that appeals to your frame of mind. Many of the pics are scans of adult cartoons containing bad language and cartoon sex and nudity.

Cool Games Nothing to do with humour at all, but the games are there if you have some time to kill.

The naughty jokes are quite funny but the rest of the site seems to be dedicated to picking up revenue from advertisers.

comedy

overall rating:	★ ★ ★ ★
classification:	homepage
updated:	monthly
navigation:	★ ★ ★ ★ ★
content:	★ ★ ★ ★
readability:	★ ★ ★ ★ ★
speed:	★ ★ ★ ★

AUS   18

http://www.nylon.net
Nylon.net

An awful lot of work has gone into this site. Some of it is very clever and some of it so misguided that you wonder if you shouldn't send someone round to see if the owner's alright. It's pointed out straight away that if you've got a thing for the stockings variety of 'nylons', you've made a mistake and need a different sort of guide altogether. But if you're in the mood for some satire, some silliness and some great variety and originality, then you've done rather well for yourself. Don't be fooled by the links running down the page, they look like they're going to take you to other sites but all the different sections are maintained by Nylon.net. Conveniently, there's also a brief description of what you'll get, so if you don't fancy it, don't click it. The design is simple, which helps to keep the page downloads quick. But it's the variety that makes this site stand out and its written in a snappy, friendly style that really works. One warning, though: there is the odd unpleasant photo on the site, so be prepared to go 'urrgh!'.

SPECIAL FEATURES

Nylonacola An excellent parody of the promotional campaigns for soft drinks. Its satire content is higher than the drink's sugar level. Very clever but with a few unpleasant images.

Rufus Porter: Mule Artist So ridiculous it almost should be real. Another parody of the real world. Rufus paints the same mule in slightly different ways. Great, useless fun.

A Reliable History of the World An extremely well-written account of important events in the world's history. It has some very funny musings but becomes more and more cynical to the point where the humour runs out. There are some very poignant messages here, but some may find the later stages, although fairly honest, a bit disturbing.

Bad Poetry Not only is the writing dreadful, but the poor poet is forced to endure a gruelling, sometimes pedantic assassination of their grammar, spelling, themes and content.

OTHER FEATURES

Anti-discrimination Law In these days of equality, here's a pertinent essay that has been missing from the political correctness debates. For the first time, someone stands up for the stupid, ugly, clumsy and incompetent. Gets you thinking.

Reasons to be Cheerful A couple of funny, if not tasteless, news items that are meant to put a smile on your face. Some do. Some don't. Updated every now and then.

Hug a Nuke Another conversation laced with satire and just begging some people to get annoyed. In the end it's pointless but funny. Unlike a real nuclear war head, which is pointy at the front and not all that funny.

Humour you have to think about. Makes a nice change out there in cyber-space, but it's not for those with an allergy to irony, sarcasm or cutting satire.

comedy

overall rating:	★ ★ ★ ★
classification:	homepage
updated:	not
navigation:	★ ★ ★ ★ ★
content:	★ ★ ★ ★
readability:	★ ★ ★ ★
speed:	★ ★ ★

UK

http://spanky.cc/index.shtml
Spanky's World

People are always claiming that the internet needs greater regulation, and after looking at this site for a few minutes you'll see why. This is a ridiculous, infantile, stupid, waste of space, which has no point or purpose, but, if you're not feeling too serious, you might just love it. Spanky's an onion head who's run away from home to get away from her horrible brother, Sparky. All the links are there on the first page, and you click at your own risk. Some of the pages are a bit sluggish, which can become a bit of a pain. Thankfully, it doesn't seem to be updated anymore.

SPECIAL FEATURES

Feel you're spending too much time on the web? Try the NetoDerm patches. Just print them from the page and stick them to your head. You know you want to.

Meet Spanky To you she might just look like a badly drawn onion head without a body, but no, she's got opinions, likes and dislikes. Find out here.

Torture Sparky Hurt her brother. He's another onion head and probably deserves it.

IQ Test Daft questions. Daft answers. Daft? Yes.

Bounce O Matic Possibly the stupidest thing in the world. But it'll make you smile. Probably.

OTHER FEATURES

Ask Spanky You've probably seen this before, it's a random answer generator. Funny if it's your first time. Not, if not.

Play the Gottcha Game One word of advice: don't.

So stupid, so mad, so ludicrous, so what are you waiting for?

comedy

overall rating: ★ ★ ★ ★	
classification: homepage	
updated: daily	
navigation: ★ ★ ★ ★ ★	
content: ★ ★ ★ ★	
readability: ★ ★ ★ ★	
speed: ★ ★ ★	
US	

http://www.amused.com
The Centre for the Easily Amused

'The Ultimate Guide to Wasting Time Online' is how this site classes itself – and if the front page is anything to go by they might be right. Hours of wasted time ahead. Sooner or later you'll realise that each colourful icon is also a link to the title that appears under the television. Once you're inside the site, the same links are available down the left of the page. The site is occasionally sluggish when loading pages, but makes up for it by being really funny. Honestly. It's updated frequently, so keep your eye on the New Stuff section.

SPECIAL FEATURES

Columns A variety of odd thoughts and musings from some slightly off-the-wall columnists. Highly recommended are Chocolate Covered Musings and Ask Snee. I hate to admit it, but just about everything here is worth reading and laughing at.

Classics Loads of Amuse-O-Matics, which are those odd things where you are prompted to input information which is then inserted into another page which becomes personalised with the things you wrote. T

Of the assorted other stuff, among the best are The Stress Relief Aquarium, where you vent your frustrations on a cute, harmless cartoon fish, and the Crash Test Dumbass, which is another great way to vent your frustration without the threat of legal action.

The personality tests might raise a smile; just answer a few questions to find out about the real you.

Amusements A few of the features double up here, but from what's new you'll lose whole weeks of your life downloading everything just to see what it's like. Unfortunately, some of the stuff isn't worth the wait. Where you will certainly waste a lot of time is in the GameScene, where, for starters, Peanut Butter and Jelly Wars is a fun change to the board game Othello. Something Fishy will get you addicted, especially when you see how high the High Scores are and try to beat them.

OTHER FEATURES

Community There's a page to meet pen pals and moderated chat rooms if you have something to say. You can even download software to send voice messages to people, subscribe to a couple of newsletters and take part in an online survey. There's also the usual guestbook and e-cards to send to your friends.

Links An excellent collection of links. They're sorted into groups, so if you want Random Silliness or Sites of Dubious Taste, you can quickly get there without any hassle.

Free Stuff Another place to sign up for newsletters, send cards, enter contests and even print out your own membership card, for fun purposes only.

Something for everyone here, and loads of variety makes it well worth visiting whenever boredom starts to raise its weary head.

comedy

overall rating: ★ ★ ★ ★	
classification: homepage	
updated: daily	
navigation: ★ ★ ★ ★ ★	
content: ★ ★ ★ ★	
readability: ★ ★ ★ ★	
speed: ★ ★ ★ ★ ★	
US	

http://www.jokefairy.com
The Joke Fairy

The Joke Fairy is like having your own huge joke book at your disposal 24 hours a day. This site features mainly short jokes so you know pretty quickly whether it's your kind of gag. There are also lots and lots of old-fashioned corny gags and puns, so there's probably something here for every occasion. The site is split up into simple sections containing hundreds of jokes. Most of them are suitable for comedians of all ages, but if you want something a little bit more risqué, have a look at the Naughty jokes section. The links on the left take you to the humour pages of your choice, where each joke has a title; click the title to see the joke. Plain white page backgrounds and few graphics mean you can get to jokes really quickly, and every joke gives you the option of sending it directly to a friend. You might end up sending a lot, as the site is updated every day.

SPECIAL FEATURES

j.o.d. archives If you want more than the single joke of the day on the first page, click here to read archives which stretch back over a six month period.

New Jokes If you're a regular to the site you'll want to be kept up to date with the newest jokes. Conveniently, the jokes are separated into Clean and Naughty, so you've been warned.

Cartoons Rather than masses of cartoons from all sorts of artists, here you get the work from just five. It's a far better way of looking at cartoons, especially if you find someone whose style you really like. Many of the jokes are the type you might find on greetings cards. Each cartoonist has thumbnails of their work and a link to their own homepage.

OTHER FEATURES

Amazing Facts Did you know that Coca-Cola was originally green? Each click brings you a new fact. Some are funny and some are not, but it's a painless way to top up your supply of useless information.

Karaoke Links to sites where you can embarrass your friends and family by singing badly, at the top of your voice, in the comfort of your own home.

Limericks (Naughty) The kind of joke you can make up yourself. Heed the warning, because some of the limericks are not for the easily offended.

Links There are hundreds of links to some outrageously silly and sometimes hysterical humour pages here. See entry in Just Browsing section.

Virtual Links to all sorts of virtual silliness, from virtual dogs to virtual vomit. Almost without exception, it's an amusing and bizarre pile of nonsense.

Lots of laughs and even more groans. A simple site with humour for everyone.

comedy

overall rating: ★ ★ ★ ★	
classification: homepage	
updated: daily	
navigation: ★ ★ ★ ★	
content: ★ ★ ★ ★	
readability: ★ ★ ★ ★ ★	
speed: ★ ★ ★ ★ ★	
US	

http://www.totallyuselessfacts.com
Totally Useless Facts

Everyone loves trivia but this site gives you more. It offers you the chance to impress friends and associates by dropping slivers of information into conversations and impressing the hell out of those listening. This site has a huge mountain of information that you didn't even know you didn't know. Half way down the page you'll find a link for a random useless fact. If you'd like to be more selective in your choice of trivia, keep going down to the bottom of the front page and click the link Take Me to the Facts. You arrive at their 'library', where you can get more random facts or browse by whatever subject takes your fancy. You get one fact to a page, occasionally backed up with a relevant picture and/or a connected piece of trivia. You'll soon notice that not all the facts are hugely funny, and the site is not without the occasional mistake, but they are all weird, fun and enjoyable to read. The site is updated daily so you're never far from a brand new useless fact.

SPECIAL FEATURES

Jesus and Elvis – Shared Facts   Ridiculous but funny comparisons that are not intended to offend.

Law   Some excellent, and mainly funny, laws. Most of these are American.

There's nothing as interesting as a fact, nothing so amusing as a completely useless fact. Fascinating and funny.

http://www.bogbeast.com
Bogbeast.com

This is a bit like Joe Cartoon, but not as good. When you're made to wait for the homepage of a site to download, you know you're going to be in for some long waits with the links inside. And you are. After a while the animations for the 'loading' screen become really irritating, but I guess it's better than looking at a blank page. The front page has just had some funky music added, which thankfully can be turned off. Some of the humour is equally annoying in its pointlessness. There are the odd big laughs for a narrow group of site visitors.

You navigate using the links just below the main page animation. Infuriatingly, the site even has a sluggish response when using the back button. Much of the content can be loaded straight onto your computer.

SPECIAL FEATURES

Fatty is a grotesquely huge, bug-eyed, hairy, nearly naked, yellow bloke. See him in all manner of guises. All the links lean towards 'No, Granny, stay away from that!', and are unsuitable for people who are offended easily. There's the occasional game thrown in amongst episodes of Fatty 'doing things'.

Bruce This short, crash-helmet-wearing annoyance, with his fixed brace and all the add-ons that go with problem teeth, has

overall rating:	★ ★ ★
classification:	homepage
updated:	occasionally
navigation:	★ ★ ★ ★ ★
content:	★ ★ ★
readability:	★ ★ ★ ★
speed:	★ ★
US	

as many clickable links as Fatty. But you'll be hard pushed to find anything to raise a smile; he's just not a funny character.

Guru Ask the Guru any yes or no question you like, and from his mountain top hideaway, he'll reveal all. Quite funny at first but the joke wears thin.

Earl This poor guy is very green and about to be sick. You can choose what his most recent meal was and I'm sure you can guess what happens next. It's colourful, if nothing else. A small percentage of readers will find it very funny.

Games Various interactive games from other bits of the site, so some of them might already be familiar. More daft than playable, and after one or two goes you'll be looking elsewhere for something new.

OTHER FEATURES

Downloads For your convenience, all the downloads are here in one place, and available for pc or Mac. Further down the page you can find links to some fairly good Screensavers featuring the characters from the site.

Join Bogbeast You can sign up for the occasional newsletter here, which keeps you updated with what's new at Bogbeast. Just click the button.

Bogbeast tries very hard and will be loved by some but passed over by more.

OTHER SITES OF INTEREST

Animated Critterlinks
http://funlinked.com/critter

The first time you come across these 'dancing' pages they can leave you feeling a little 'eh?'. For some this feeling never goes away. But for those of you who like tinny music and themed graphics that spin round and 'dance', here is the perfect place for you to dwell on your strange interest. If nothing else, they should raise a smile. I think you have to have a certain respect for someone who gets up in the morning and says 'Today, I'm going to make a donut spin round to music!'. It's just one of those 'internet' things. Don't look for explanations, just get in there and enjoy. For some reason that can't be explained, Monster Mash is a personal favourite.

Comedyzine.com
http://www.comedyzine.com

Fairly middle of the road American comedy site. There's an enormous archive of political humour, updated regularly, as well as a regular columnist, amusing to-do lists, photos, comic tirades about everything. May well be a little too American for some tastes.

Crack Shack
http://www.heff.net/crackshack

Sometimes there's no comparison between cartoons and actual funny photographs. The real thing is always funnier. So here we have an American collection of real photos, the occasional one is 'doctored', but most are authentic. A lot of them are very funny, but the occasional one dips its toe into the pond of 'downright disturbing'. Unfortunately there are no thumbnails, so you only have the image name as a guide to what you're going to get. It's a fairly ugly site, but the photos are funny enough to make it worth your while.

FunPlanet
http://www.funplanet.co.uk

There are some great fun games to play, especially if you like catching sheep and cat jumping. There are some quizzes, chat and the chance to win prizes. All the content is played online, so there's not much time spent waiting for downloads. Another site to amuse even the most bored mind.

Gags and Pranks
http://www.geocities.com/netsur24/index.html

If you're the sort of person who likes to play jokes on family and friends, there's lots here to keep you amused. Basically it's a list of small programmes that give the appearance of altering the way your computer behaves. You can make the mouse act strangely, create very real looking error windows, or even make it look like your friend's computer is wiping their hard disc. Don't panic though, they're all perfectly safe, but the recipient doesn't know that! There's lots to choose from, depending on how nasty you're feeling.

Joke Post
http://www.jokepost.com

This is as close to an online encyclopaedia of jokes as you

can find on the internet. The gags are split up into easily recognisable sections, such as blondes, doctors, relationships and so on, so if you want something specific it is easy to find. There are masses of jokes, all sent in by people like you, and not altered in any way. So, knowing what people tend to be like, you can expect to find some fairly bad taste stuff. Only the jokes containing bad language are filtered out into the Uncensored area.

OXymoron
http://paul.merton.ox.ac.uk
Nothing to do with the comedian Paul Merton. This is, instead, a site run by some of the members of Merton College Oxford University. It's a really good collection of humour from around the net. It's got good pages of categorised jokes, and lots of comedy lists like 'Why Coffee is Better than Men' as well as funny stories and the sort of written humour that gets sent round offices, then around friends, then around the world. Lots to choose from. Lots of laughs.

The Funny Farm
http://www.geocities.com/Heartland/Hills/3456/index.html
The Funny Farm is a simply wonderful list of comedy items. There are no jokes here as such, just some very funny pieces of humour. These are more of the sorts of things that get sent round offices and the internet. You'll probably have seen a few of them before, but having them all collected together in one place is just perfect. From things like 'Preparations for Parenthood' and 'Tips from the Horror Movie Survival Guide', to

'Creative Ways to Say Someone is Stupid' parts one and two. There's a fairly big comedy archive too, and an occasional mailing list to join.

Wibble.org
http://www.wibble.org

Similar to The Funny Farm, Wibble has just collected together some really funny stuff. There are some long jokes and a collection of Bad jokes, but on the whole these are more funny lists, reasons why and collections of comic advice, musings and general silliness. There is something for everyone. And you don't even need to worry too much about offensive content as the iffy ones are all collected together under Possibly Offensive for you to avoid, or go straight towards, according to your preference. It's nothing but nonsense, but very funny.

plain stupid

With all the wonderful things that you can now learn and achieve by using the internet, why do so many people abuse this potential for doing something really worthwhile? It's like people who get a dictionary and can't help but look up all the rude words. They miss the point entirely.

However, as they exercise their right to waste their lives in whatever ridiculous and silly way they see fit, some of these people have succeeded in creating very funny pages. They may be pointless, yes. These people might have too much time on their hands. Absolutely. But who cares? The world's too serious as it is. These people are great. They are the bringers of laughter. Just hope they never end up dating your sister.

comedy

overall rating: ★★★★★	
classification: homepage	
updated: monthly	
navigation: ★★★★★	
content: ★★★★★	
readability: ★★★★★	
speed: ★★★★	
US	

http://www.darwinawards.com
Darwin Awards

This site celebrates 'Charles Darwin's theory of evolution by commemorating the remains of those who improved our gene pool by removing themselves from it'. Basically, if you did something really stupid that brought about your own demise, your story could well be featured here. These are not fictional but actual stories of how people ended up dying. Sounds a little macabre? Well, it probably is, but most of these stories are so funny that you don't really think about it. The site is huge, getting around a quarter of a million visitors a month, which unfortunately means some of the pages are slow to appear.

However, the site relies heavily on people like you sending in your newspaper stories and is keen for everyone to vote on the regular issues posted on the site, and, of course, to vote for each story to see if it's worthy of the coveted Darwin Award itself. The site links are in the left-hand frame, which is always there, wherever you click. Enjoy.

SPECIAL FEATURES

Darwin Awards See the awards year by year and read the current batch of human stupidity just begging to pick up an award. You can choose the titles from the left hand frame or simply click the Next button beneath the story to go to the next one.

Honorable Mentions The people in these stories stopped short of actually killing themselves, but deserve a mention for the intellectually challenged genes they carry.

Urban Legends You may well have come across some of these stories of misfortune, but rest assured, these are not true, no matter how much someone tells you they happened to a friend of a friend.

Personal Accounts Not all the stories need to be found in papers; some of them might actually have happened to you personally or in your vicinity. Here, some people retell appalling moments of abject stupidity they witnessed or were guilty of.

Slush Pile This is where you'll find all the newest submissions that have not yet been categorised or checked for authenticity. This, however, does not make them any less funny than the rest of the site.

Philosophy Forum Absolutely enormous notice boards to discuss a variety of issues, from the awards themselves to Religion and General Philosophy discussions. These are lively and very often intelligent discussions, as ordinary people have their say.

Newsletter Have Darwin Awards and other stories of deadly stupidity delivered to your email box twice a month, for nothing.

Lots of people find the stories and the whole idea of Darwin Awards distasteful and inappropriate, but maybe those people just take life too seriously. This is a hideously amusing site. Enough said.

comedy

overall rating:	★ ★ ★ ★ ★
classification:	homepage
updated:	daily
navigation:	★ ★ ★ ★ ★
content:	★ ★ ★ ★ ★
readability:	★ ★ ★
speed:	★ ★ ★ ★ ★
UK	

http://www.cs.man.ac.uk/~hancockd/dwol.htm
Dave's Web of Lies

So you thought the internet was a bastion of honesty and integrity? Don't be so silly. Lies abound, and here at Dave's Web of Lies, you can read some of the simplest, funniest humour to be found anywhere. For instance, did you realise that 'the longest (and also, paradoxically, the shortest) word in the English language is 'badger'. It's a very simple black on white site that let's the content do the talking instead of spending a single second longer on design than is absolutely necessary. Navigate around using the tabs at the top of the opening page.

SPECIAL FEATURES

Lie of the Day Read a single lie a day, or click the Lie Of The Day By Mail link, follow the instructions and have lies delivered by email to read at your convenience. And that's absolutely true.

A Week of Lies A single lie is never quite enough, so why not check out the last seven days of lies?

Database of Lies Maybe you're speaking at a wedding or at the United Nations and you want an appropriate lie for the occasion. No problem. The database currently holds more than 3000 lies; you can search by topic, by the name of the liar who submitted it, or alphabetically.

Celebrity Liar Stephen Fry shares some of his favourite lies. Whether Mr Fry even knows about this page is not clear, but if it is just another lie, who cares?

Submit a Lie Get involved and send the site your best ever lie. Hopefully it'll be better than the one about why you hadn't done your homework back in the first year at school.

There's something very pleasing about words that are not anchored in the real world. The words on this site are often funny, sometimes clever and absolutely always complete fibs.

comedy

overall rating: ★ ★ ★ ★ ★	
classification: reference	
updated: weekly	
navigation: ★ ★ ★ ★ ★	
content: ★ ★ ★ ★ ★	
readability: ★ ★ ★ ★ ★	
speed: ★ ★ ★ ★ ★	
US	

http://www.dumblaws.com
Dumb Laws

You listen to them promising you the world, you take your pick and then you vote for the people who are going to help make everything alright again. Then they come up with the ridiculous laws featured here. This is a very funny site that has a huge list of stupid and ridiculous laws. Many have been certified as authentic; some have been collected from around the net without verification. Don't let that reduce your enjoyment of a site that makes the belief that we are the most intelligent, well-organised species on the planet seem very doubtful.

This is a very easy site to get around. There are links on the left and more detailed descriptions of the same links running down the middle of the main page. It's updated at least once a week. Dumb Laws is part of the Dumb Network, so when you're finished here why not check out some other dumb things. Use the links down the bottom of the left-hand side.

SPECIAL FEATURES

United States Each state can be viewed in all its dumb law glory. The American laws considerably outnumber the ones from anywhere else in the world, which could be because it's a huge country, the site is based in the USA and the laws are easier to find, or for some other reason. You decide.

Other Countries It's not just America; the rest of the world is completely bonkers too. For instance, apparently in England it is illegal for a lady to eat chocolates on a public conveyance; in Scotland it is illegal to be drunk in possession of a cow and in France you cannot call your own pig Napoleon. Now you know.

Random Law If you don't care which country's Government you laugh at, try this random law generator.

Some silly people who post to the site get very irate because some of the laws may not be true. True or not, this is a very funny site which is there to be enjoyed and not taken too seriously.

comedy

http://www.emotioneric.com
Eric Conveys an Emotion

Eric conveys an emotion. Half the world go 'yeah, and...?' while the other half fall off their chairs and run the risk of drowning in tears of their own laughter. Even Eric admits that the site is fairly pointless and yet it generates several thousand visitors a week. What's it all about then? Well, Eric posts pictures of himself, performing emotions as requested by site visitors. So, taking it from the top of the left hand column, if you were to click on Happiness, Sadness, Anger, or Fear, Eric would appear in the centre of the screen pulling his version of the emotion. Not very interesting? But wait, scroll down a little further and the emotions become far more amusing. Falling Down Stairs, Realising That You Are Superior To Everything On The Planet and My Foot Is On Fire are only three of the dozens available to you. Only now do you realise that you have arrived at a special place where normality, maturity and importance have not lived for some time. However, you will laugh, and if you don't there may well be something seriously wrong with you.

The links to the emotions are on the left, proposed emotions Eric might tackle in the future, when he's got time, are down the right, and other links are highlighted in white at the bottom.

SPECIAL FEATURES
Request The all-important section where you can challenge Eric

to perform an emotion of your choosing. If you get stuck, have another look at the proposed emotions on the right for a little inspiration.

About Interesting to discover that the site is not in fact coming straight from a padded cell, but from a guy with a job and, occasionally, a life.

Guaranteed to cheer up the gloomiest afternoon. Best used as a 'dip-in' site; overuse on any given day may well result in your face permanently becoming set in Eric's portrayal of Senile Dementia.

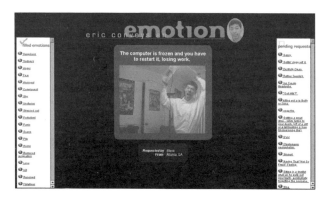

comedy

overall rating: ★ ★ ★ ★ ★	
classification: ezine	
updated: daily?	
navigation: ★ ★ ★ ★ ★	
content: ★ ★ ★ ★	
readability: ★ ★ ★ ★ ★	
speed: ★ ★ ★ ★ ★	
UK	

http://www.emporiumoffruit.co.uk
The Emporium of Fruit

From the first page you may think that The Emporium of Fruit is a mad cult whose members have to smile a lot and wear jumpers hand-knitted by ageing maiden aunts; who knows, maybe it is. However, it is funny. Very. To see what's in store in this odd but well designed site, simply click the words next to the happy, smiling people and Bob's your Uncle, you're inside. The Emporium is an ezine kind of thing with fabricated stories and scathing attacks, laced with biting, twisted and sarcastic humour that will have you laughing, or praying you never move house and end up next to these guys.

They claim it's updated every day, but this appears to be lies; one post to the message board claims they simply recycle the content by rotating the same articles. But there's still some excellent content to enjoy first time round. Bits of it will be found offensive by some people.

SPECIAL FEATURES

Today's Issue There are Features and Regulars to enjoy. Recent features have covered a viciously amusing attack on pop sensations Steps, a review of the Dennis Hopper Action Bear, and Desktop Hell, where you can download wallpaper for your computer that is both funny and offensive to some. In the Regulars section you can find Satan's Jukebox, which plays horrible lounge and life music while you browse; the option to send in details of your Keith Chegwin sightings ('Don't do it for yourself. Do it for the sake of your children.'); and, of course, the ever-popular, and completely fictional, Celebrity Q & A.

Shop @emporium Products you can't actually buy, but wouldn't the world be an amazing place if you could?

Help Funny rather than helpful. Covers such areas as 'I don't see anything on my monitor', 'I don't feel well' and 'Why isn't murder legal yet?'

Certainly not humour for everyone. But if it's to your taste, you'll eat here till you're sick.

comedy

overall rating: ★ ★ ★ ★	
classification: homepage	
updated: fortnightly	
navigation: ★ ★ ★ ★ ★	
content: ★ ★ ★	
readability: ★ ★ ★ ★	
speed: ★ ★ ★	
CAN	

http://www.funlinked.com/critter
Animated Critterlinks

Imagine the scene, you take perfectly normal, healthy people, and cut off the top of their heads using an ice-cream scoop. Then, in a perfectly humane way, replace their brains with a small cheese salad, pop the top back on and see what happens. Well, what happens is people create the pages covered by this site. They get it into their lettuce leaf heads that 'dance' pages are the way forward. If you have never experienced these type of pages before you might like to put newspaper down on the floor first, use round-edged scissors and make sure you have an adult on hand to help you. Basically, very tinny music plays, and cartoons and photos dance. Badly. But sometimes they manage to be funny. It's impossible to put your finger on quite why.

Click any of the titles in any of the boxes. Some of the pages take a while to load because of the animations and sound files. Frighteningly, this site is updated every two weeks.

SPECIAL FEATURES
Dancing Critters Basically, 'things' dance. Cartoons, animals, flowers, vampires. Anything really. The purple smiley faces are supposed to lead you to the best pages, but it's rather subjective. Try Stray Cat Strut for an immediate experience of these dancing page phenomena.

Dancin' People You guessed it, 'people' dance. The Prince

Charles page is very funny, as is the Dancing Clinton, which also features our very own Tony Blair.

Miscellaneous Dances Everything else. Generally even more substandard than usual.

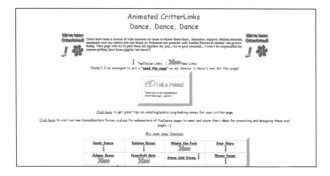

You have to experience things like this to be a fully rounded human being... no you don't. You may laugh, you may fall asleep with boredom, or you might replace your brain with salad and make one yourself.

overall rating:	★ ★ ★ ★
classification:	homepage
updated:	occasionally
navigation:	★ ★ ★
content:	★ ★ ★ ★
readability:	★ ★ ★
speed:	★ ★ ★ ★
US	

http://www.badart.com
Bad Art.com

In this world of unkindness, greed and jealousy, there is nothing that gives us more pleasure than pointing the finger at those who are supremely awful at something. Pointing the finger and laughing till we feel sick. This is a site that points, jumps up and down and screams: 'You have no artistic talent at all!' The site has actually paid small amounts of money for the tat on show, as part of a bizarre and growing community of people online who actually like Bad Art.

The site is basic in design, but the reproduction of the art is good. Unfortunately it hasn't been updated for a while, although new stuff is expected soon. The links are on the left of the first page and there are some vague features as you scroll down. Prepare to be amazed, for your mouth to open slightly and for spittle to possibly dribble down your chin.

SPECIAL FEATURES

The Gallery Dozens of appalling paintings. Each one can be clicked for a full size viewing and a short comment on their particular lack of merit.

Ramblings Do you think it's easy being a connoisseur of Bad Art? Read some of the trials of traipsing around markets trying to find suitable additions to your collection and the occasional letter of disapproval from critics of the site.

Bad Links This is where it starts to get scary. Here are links to other people who keep collections of dreadful art online, for further pointing and laughing.

Artists have spent time and money producing what this site now ridicules, which seems right, fitting and the only thing to do.

comedy

overall rating: ★ ★ ★ ★	
classification: homepage	
updated: occasionally	
navigation: ★ ★ ★ ★ ★	
content: ★ ★ ★	
readability: ★ ★ ★ ★	
speed: ★ ★ ★ ★ ★	
US	

http://www.pcola.gulf.net/~irving/bunnies/index.html
Bunny Survival Tests Homepage

Marshmallow Bunnies volunteer for a series of tests to determine their own strengths and weaknesses. Yep, you read the last sentence right – Bunnies. On a simple, but pinkish site, you too can see the results of these experiments. It doesn't seem to be updated very often, but you might find that what's here is enough to satisfy your cravings for knowledge. After the introduction are the links to the experiments themselves. After that, just keep scrolling down the page for the rest.

A great deal of thought and possibly misguided effort went into these tests, so make sure that you give them the serious consideration they deserve. Mark Smith, whose site this is, states on every single page how the information is copyrighted and cannot be copied without written permission. It's a hugely silly site, reasonably funny, but who on earth would want to pinch bits of it?

SPECIAL FEATURES

The experiments are all worth a look, for reasons which are not immediately, if ever, clear. The Coyote Test is particularly silly, while the Flame Tolerance Test is particularly gruesome. All the tests are written up in a lively scientific research kind of way, which just makes them funnier.

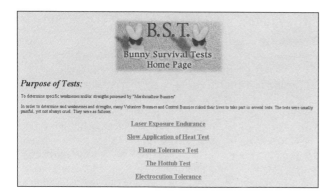

Traitor Bunny Brief but funny report and picture, detailing what happens to a marshmallow bunny who is found guilty of selling out his own kind.

Mini-Bunny-FAQ Quite amusing in themselves, but most important is the link to The Bunnies Strike Back, which takes you to a sister site detailing what happened when the Bunnies got their revenge on the evil Peeps, which are a kind of confectionery we don't get in Britain. Very daft.

Very odd. Genius? Madman? It's a thin line.

comedy

overall rating: ★★★★
classification: homepage
updated: occasionally
navigation: ★★★★★
content: ★★★★
readability: ★★★★★
speed: ★★★★★
UK

http://www.cloudkissing.com
Cloud Kissing

As soon as you read the Company Profile on the first page you will realise that this is a real company that produces real clouds. This is a humorous look at a company that's been around for millions of years, producing clouds for the mass market. It's harmless, funny and absolutely barking mad, with interesting ideas for clouds for all occasions. The links are on the left and take you to all sorts of cloud-related lunacy. It's updated about once a month, so remember to pop back and see what's new in the big business of clouds. And if you start to believe in all this, lock yourself in a cupboard until the feelings go away.

SPECIAL FEATURES

Book a Cloud Thanks to Saint Peter, it is now possible to book your own cloud for that time that comes to us all when we must take our place in the big internet madhouse in the sky. Make sure you're honest about how good you've been.

Rent a Cloud Proof that when you're depressed and convinced a big cloud is following you around, it probably is.

Plague of Frogs Not content with just cloud purchases, you can also order a typical plague of frogs. It's the perfect end to any outdoor event.

Message Board Stay in the spirit of the site, as funny posts make it onto the site for all to read.

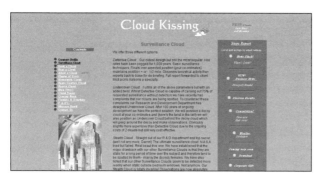

A really imaginative humour trips merrily through this site. With a bit more depth it could become a cult site for those who like gentle rather than aggressive or obscene humour.

comedy

overall rating:	★ ★ ★ ★
classification:	information
updated:	weekly
navigation:	★ ★ ★ ★
content:	★ ★ ★ ★
readability:	★ ★ ★ ★
speed:	★ ★ ★ ★ ★
US	

http://humormatters.com
Humor Matters

As you are pottering around the internet, laughing at comedy sites, you may not have realised how much good you are doing yourself. This site explains it all. Run by the President of the American Association for Therapeutic Humor, it's dedicated to the use of humour in psychotherapy and the treatment of patients with a range of conditions. Obviously set up as a resource for people who work in the field of Therapeutic Humour. Now before you start to fall asleep, this site does not read like an academic textbook; it has serious articles, but also jokes, bumper stickers, and all manner of funny bits and pieces. It's very easy to get around; there are five columns, each headed with what you'll find beneath. It's a very interesting and also very funny site. Jokes are updated weekly, other additions once a month.

SPECIAL FEATURES

Funny Stuff All the stuff you would expect to find on a humour site. There are jokes, quotes and funny news stories.

Topical Humour As well as sections dedicated to Seasonal humour, there are funny collections of daft things kids say, language and age-related humour.

Information This is the serious stuff. Articles on laughter as, literally, a medicine and how to use it in our lives. There are details of conferences and an interesting FAQ section which discusses the very nature of Humour.

Resources More serious content. A biography of Steven M. Sultanoff, the man who runs the site; comedy-related items to buy, for those working with humour as a clinical treatment; and more links.

This informative site not only makes us laugh, which we now know is good for us; it also explains why humour really matters.

comedy

overall rating: ★★★★	
classification: homepage	
updated: frequently	
navigation: ★★★★★	
content: ★★★★	
readability: ★★★★	
speed: ★★★★★	

http://rock.jackal.org
Rock Home Page

Bad news for surfers who think they've found a site dedicated to Rock Music in a humorous and entertaining way. This is about Rock. And not just any old rock, like stone or granite, but the one and only 'Rock'. You'll get the idea once you're inside.

It's designed like a normal fan site, with many of the expected features, plus the added bonus of a live Rock Cam of the Rock himself. Under this link are 10 more that take you to different areas of the site. At the bottom is where you can sign up for the weekly newsletter. It's a clever idea which upsets people by its very simplicity. But take it in good faith, and laugh. It's updated every few seconds, via the Rock Cam.

SPECIAL FEATURES

About Rock Not sure what's going on here? Missing the point? Click here to get into the swing of things.

Frequently Asked Questions I'm sure most people have questions when they've visited this site. Some nice, some decidedly unfriendly. This section deals with each question in a mature, adult and very funny way.

Rock Cam Every five seconds this web cam gives you the very latest on your hero and mine, Rock.

'The Best of' Rock Gallery Since the Rock Cam archive has had to be closed down due to excess traffic, this is where the best Rock photos can be found. There's a large selection. If you sign up for the newsletter you'll get access to exclusive photos.

Amateur Nude Photos Parents and people of a sensitive nature need not worry that explicit photos are about to be seen. So long as pictures of naked rocks don't bother you, there's nothing to worry about.

Pointlessly funny. It will have you laughing and feeling childish, but jolly, for doing so.

comedy

overall rating: ★ ★ ★ ★	
classification: homepage	
updated: occasionally	
navigation: ★ ★ ★ ★ ★	
content: ★ ★ ★ ★	
readability: ★ ★ ★ ★	
speed: ★ ★ ★ ★	
US	

http://www.rockschool.com
Rock School

Ever wondered what it's really like in a rock band? Ever wanted to know what the pitfalls are and how to avoid them? This site provides a tongue-in-cheek look at everything you need to know to be a rock musician. It's probably most rewarding to those who have experienced the trials of being in a band themselves, but is still amusing to everyone else.

The lessons are given via streaming video clips which have great sound but fairly ordinary animation. The earlier lessons are in the form of interactive cartoons. The main three links are on the left, highlighted with delightful, no-hope head-bangers so you don't get lost. New lessons are added every couple of months.

SPECIAL FEATURES

Lessons Very informative lessons that will teach you, among other things, not to leave unfinished lyrics lying around, the benefits of supporting a much bigger band than yourselves, and understanding how being in a band can affect your relationships with women. All the animations feature our three hapless rockers, who are dull enough to give even the least talented musician hope and optimism.

Activities It's not only lessons that need to be learned, skills also need to be honed. This section provides interactive training to improve such necessary talents as getting a gig for the band, improving your musical skills with the Song-O-Meter, and, of course, navigating through a maze of corridors trying to get to the toilet on time.

Basics/Exam The Basics are text-based advice, which after the previous animations are not as entertaining. The Exam is a humorous, multiple choice quiz that rates your chances of making it in the world of Rock.

A very entertaining, themed humour site. Nice to see comedy and originality head-banging, hand in hand.

comedy

overall rating: ★ ★ ★ ★	
classification: homepage	
updated: not	
navigation: ★ ★ ★ ★ ★	
content: ★ ★ ★ ★	
readability: ★ ★ ★ ★ ★	
speed: ★ ★ ★ ★ ★	
US	

http://www.rinkworks.com/dialect
The Dialectizer

There is absolutely no point to this page. It serves no useful purpose and does not necessarily help to make the world a better place. But, you have to admit, there's something extremely funny about reading something terribly ordinary and then applying the Dialectizer and reading it again in Cockney, Redneck or even Moron. You may feel this is a little too infantile for your tastes, but that could simply be a sign that your underwear is a little too tight and you need to get out more. It's a very simple, one-page site; keep scrolling down the page and you get to the end and there is no more. Any clickable links are blue, and the final third of the page is dedicated to disclaimers, how it works and links to other associated sites. This is an almost finished project and, apart from two or three additional dialects, there will be no more updates.

SPECIAL FEATURES

Dialectize a Web Page Simply choose a dialect from the drop down box, write a web address in the next box and click Dialectize. After a moment you will see the whole page in a new light. Try it with official pages that bore you rigid, or your own homepage. Don't worry, what you are doing will not change the site in question, it simply alters it for your viewing pleasure and only while you're at the Dialectizer Homepage.

Dialectize Text Turn anything you like into a different dialect.

Write your words in the box and hit the button. You could try
cutting and pasting annoying letters from the management or
your boss. You could even see what your homework looks like
after getting the Dialectizer treatment.

*You'll try this out, you'll laugh, you'll try it again, then send it to
your friends, then they'll try it. Everyone will have a laugh and
then you'll all sit around wondering why.*

comedy

overall rating:	★ ★ ★ ★
classification:	homepage
updated:	weekly
navigation:	★ ★ ★ ★
content:	★ ★ ★ ★
readability:	★ ★ ★ ★
speed:	★ ★ ★ ★
US	

http://www.tackymail.com/index.htm
The Tacky Postcard Archive

For proof that it isn't just on the net that absolute garbage gets created, here is a collection of the most awful postcards. They have all actually been on sale somewhere in the world at one time or another. Lovingly collected by the site owner, they are categorised for easier viewing pleasure and updated every week or so. The four main site links are in grey boxes just beneath the site title. If you want something more specific you can click on the red words under these titles. It's very simple, really. When you find an especially awful one, send it to friends and enemies alike. You just know they deserve it.

SPECIAL FEATURES

Main Galleries The Anti-tourism post cards are especially pleasing when you remember that at one time, some bloke in a suit thought these pictures would help to promote his home town. The Bad Advertising section probably saw the downfall of one or two executives and the Just Offal ones speak for themselves.

Holidays You're getting a feel for the site now and you want to send a card to a friend, but there's just too much awful stuff to choose from. Why not choose one from this seasonal range to fit the particular time of year. Or even send a Christmas postcard for Valentine's day or a Mother's Day suggestion for Father's Day. It's up to you.

Suggestions These are collected from the rest of the site and are offered to you as suggestions for when you simply can't find the perfect card. Basically, it's just more of the same.

Many of the official e-card sites offer pretty dreadful cards for you to send, but this one beats them all. Just make sure recipients have a sense of humour and realise it's just a bit of fun.

comedy

overall rating: ★ ★ ★ ★	
classification: homepage	
updated: occasionally	
navigation: ★ ★ ★ ★	
content: ★ ★ ★ ★	
readability: ★ ★ ★ ★	
speed: ★ ★ ★ ★	
UK	

http://www.fartfarm.com
Tracey's Fart Farm

What do you mean, 'adolescent nonsense shouldn't be allowed'? Come on, everyone does it. Most indulge privately or with intimate friends, but some prefer to share the experience. Who are we to deny them this release, as it were? Tracey is quite a dedicated 'wind' connoisseur and should be applauded, and quite possibly avoided after prunes or curry. Her site is populated with little men in red shorts who have certain problems that you can hear if you click them. Towards the bottom of the page there are currently 70 'bottom burps' which you can listen to for hours, if that's what you fancy. Not to be outdone, you might also like to consider sending in a sound clip of a guff of your own. Now that's got you thinking, hasn't it? The seven main links are at the top of the page. Click away for all the fun but none of the unpleasantness.

SPECIAL FEATURES

Farting Stories Firstly, do not be alarmed by the photo at the top of the page. Secondly, stories about breaking wind? Do we really need that? Unfortunately we do. It's gross, infantile nonsense that, deep down, you never grow out of. Visitors to the site have sent in their own thrilling stories. Maybe you could send in yours?

Farting Poems The funniest thing is that people actually gave up some time to write these things, and some are quite funny.

Unusual and Rude Wavs Songs and stuff to listen to. Some of it very rude and offensive. Individual files could do with better descriptions so you know what you're getting.

Crap-a-gram There will only be a few people you know who will appreciate this kind of greeting. Definitely bad taste, but then again you're supposed to read them not eat them.

It is constantly amazing to see what people use their websites for. This site is truly funny. It really shouldn't be, but it is.

comedy

overall rating:
★ ★ ★

classification:
homepage

updated:
frequently

navigation:
★ ★ ★ ★ ★

content:
★ ★ ★

readability:
★ ★

speed:
★ ★ ★ ★ ★

http://www.uio.no./~seide/naken.html
Hot Nude Pictures

You may be wondering what place nude pictures have in a guide to comedy, and why there is no adult content warning in this review. One look at the pictures involved will reveal all. There are no photos on this page, only drawings. And these drawings have no artistic merit at all and look exactly as a four-year-old might draw them. All the pictures are of famous people, but without the name attached to the drawing, so no one would know. This is nothing but harmless nonsense, and if the site owner gives any explanation for why he is inviting visitors to submit their own 'artwork' it's impossible for English speakers to tell, as the whole site is in Norwegian (we think).

From Bill Clinton to the Spice Girls, no one is safe. Click on the names down the left-hand side and maybe you'll start to understand why you or anybody you know have never been to Norway. Updated a couple of times a month.

SPECIAL FEATURES

Er, it's difficult to say if anything is 'special'. Each drawing is as silly as the next. Some are Hollywood stars, some models, and sports personalities. Simply enjoy the stupidity of it all.

One of the most ridiculous pages you are ever likely to see.

http://www.angelfire.com/mi/slackertrash
Richie's Amusement Park

Many sites tell you the screen resolution that their site is best viewed in. This site is best viewed with the top of your head cut off and your brain scooped out with a teaspoon. The basic idea is that you've arrived at an amusement park. That's where this site and reality part ways. The 'rides' and park amenities are in a list down the centre of the page, and although the wait is shorter than at a real amusement park, a lot of the pages are quite sluggish to load into your browser. Most of the links take you to visual gags where the emphasis is on 'visual' and the 'gags' are long forgotten. There are some great, tinny songs that pop up on various pages. As this is an Angelfire homepage, annoying advert windows pop up all the time. It's best to simply minimise the first window and leave it alone; otherwise, if you close the window, another opens when you go to a different page. The design is great, every page having a completely different feel to the others, but the content has been created with a sense of humour that seems to come from another galaxy, where it's obviously a capital crime to know what's funny and what isn't.

SPECIAL FEATURES

Fireside Chat Some funny words of wisdom along the lines of: 'Dad always thought laughter was the best medicine, which I guess is why several of us died of tuberculosis.'

overall rating:	★ ★ ★
classification:	homepage
updated:	occasionally
navigation:	★ ★ ★ ★ ★
content:	★ ★
readability:	★ ★ ★ ★
speed:	★ ★ ★
US	

Fun at Work A pretty funny list of things to make the working day pass more quickly, and some outrageous excuses to give when you don't go in.

There's so much to see and yet so little point. You'll leave the site with one overwhelming question: 'eh?'

OTHER SITES OF INTEREST

Comedy Butchers

http://www.comedybutchers.com

British Comedy at its silliest. Three guys decide that socialising, having friends and possibly making something of their lives is secondary when they can create some excellent comedy. They've found the 1945 version of Windows, and they've created some news in the style of Have I Got News For You around some otherwise perfectly normal photos. They've even got their own columns, sketches you can listen to online, and an absolutely hysterical Lonely Hearts page from 1943.

Karma-Sooty

http://www.karma-sooty.co.uk

18

The funniest parts of this site are the title and the idea. Sooty has needs just like everyone else, and as long as he and Sue are both consenting adult puppets, which I'm sure they are, then there are no problems. They have a full and varied adult life together and are open-minded enough to share their experiences with you. Sooty having sex, that's just got to be funny, hasn't it? Well, maybe, but once you've clicked the drop-down box and seen some of the lurid titles you can choose to view, even the most broad-minded person might find themself cringing. The site is almost certainly best viewed through an alcoholic haze, with some like-minded mates who are dropping their kebabs all over the place and giggling in a way that will embarrass them the next morning.

Magic Cybercam

http://larsplace.com/cybercam

Try out this brand new product which will take two photos of you through your computer monitor, process them in just a few moments and then show you the results. There are very simple, step-by-step instructions which mean you can't make a mistake. So, say cheese and experience the Cybercam in all its glory. It's completely free, so what have you got to lose? Then send it to your friends.

Mate in a State

http://www.mateinastate.com

Such a monumentally important site it's incredible to believe that it has only been running since April 2000. It's so simple. Your mates get drunk, fall down, embarrass themselves with haircuts and fashion problems, and you, as their caring friend, take a photo of them in their misfortune, send it to this site and the rest of us point and laugh at them. The top 10 pictures each month are voted on and the eventual winner gets a prize. The potential for revenge is enormous, but on the whole this site is about poking fun at your friends and laughing. A lot. There's nothing so funny as a mate's misfortune. But be warned, do it to them and your friends will be looking for an opportunity to do it to you. Lots of people will think this site childish and a waste of web space, but who cares, they've probably forgotten how to enjoy themselves anyway.

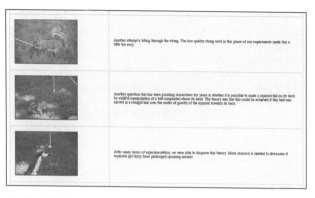

Another attempt at biting through the string. The low-quality string used in this phase of our experiments made this a little too easy.

Another question that has been puzzling researchers for years is whether it is possible to make a squirrel fall on its back by skillful manipulation of a bait suspended above its head. The theory was that this could be achieved if this bait was moved in a straight line over the center of gravity of the squirrel towards its back.

After many hours of experimentation, we were able to disprove this theory. More research is needed to determine if squirrels get dizzy from prolonged spinning around.

Squirrel Fishing
http://www.eecs.harvard.edu/~yaz/en/squirrel_fishing.html

Yep, you read it correctly. Squirrel Fishing. It's what certain Harvard types decided to call an investigation surrounding 'a new approach to rodent performance evaluation'. There are a series of pictures of the scientific study in progress, ending with the hapless squirrel hoisted into the air. Animal lovers should not be alarmed, no hooks are used and no harm comes to any bushy-tailed critter. Isn't Harvard where the best American minds are nurtured? Thought so.

The Nipple Project
http://www.cultofmarms.org/index.html

So, picture the scene. This lady, for reasons which are probably best not discussed, has planned to have her areolae redesigned. She's leaving the nipples as they are, but has invited the assorted lunatics of the internet to design the rest. Oh dear, oh dear, oh dear. Lots of people took up the challenge and the results are posted for all to see. There are patterns, cartoons and even a couple of animals and people. In mid 1999 one of these designs was chosen and the next step was to have it tattooed onto her body. Well, it's her body to do with as she sees fit, but it's her mind I think we should be worried about. There was never a better time to use the old phrase: kids, do not try this at home. If nothing else, you've got to laugh.

The World's Best Bubblewrap Homepage
http://fathom.org/opalcat/bubblewrap.html

Yep, that stuff you used to take off presents as a child and spend longer playing with than the present itself. This site is dedicated to the stuff and the art of popping it in numerous ways. Apparently Pamela Anderson rates it as a personal favourite, so make of that what you will. But, and this surely is the reason that the web is a wonderful place, there are online sheets of bubblewrap that you can happily 'pop' with your mouse. You know you want to, and you just know you're going to. And when you're all popped out, why not send in your own methods of popping so that you and the rest of the world can have an even more satisfying bubblewrap experience?

just browsing

There will be days when you're on the internet and nothing in particular catches your eye. You'll have time on your hands to do a little surfing, but you just can't think of anything you want to see. There's no point opening up a search engine if you don't have any words to look for. If only someone could take you by the hand and point you in the direction of some really good sites.

Well, for a start, you've got this guide, but we can't possibly cover everything out there that might interest you. Anyway, it's important that, at some point, you try and stand on your own two feet and take some responsibility for your own humour. Until then, what we've done is gather together some excellent sites that have gathered together some excellent sites. Pop along to any of these places and you'll be spoilt for choice. There are huge sites dealing with everything humorously imaginable. They take the hard work out of online comedy finding. Pick any of them and just click around. Alternatively, pick them all, click everything and never see your friends and family again.

comedy

overall rating: ★ ★ ★ ★ ★	
classification: links guide	
updated: frequently	
navigation: ★ ★ ★ ★ ★	
content: ★ ★ ★ ★ ★	
readability: ★ ★ ★ ★ ★	
speed: ★ ★ ★ ★ ★	
US	

http://www.bored.com/ie.html
Bored.com

If you're busy searching for something to give your funny bone a tweak, here's as good a place as any to get started. There's a good list of links to sites to tickle your fancy. There are simple 'joke' sites like One Stop Jokes, where you can enjoy gags online or have them sent to you by email. If you want a little more variety, why not try a link like LaughNet or Humour.com, which have a selection box of daft and funny stuff? Some of the sites are specifically geared to a type of humour, such as That Was Stupid, which oddly enough is based on stupid people doing stupid things. And, as the majority of the internet is populated by people with way too much time on their hands, there are also the pages which are just plain daft. Try out Create a Fart, which, without the aid of beans, produces something that's neither big nor clever.

Follow the links down the page until you find something you fancy, click it, and kiss goodbye to your sensible, mature nature. Come back often, as it's updated a couple of times a week.

When you've looked through all the links, go to the bottom and Bored.com supplies you with more pages to laugh at.

A fantastic place to get started in the world of internet humour.

http://www.comedy-zone.net
Comedy Zone

If you can think of something, anything, that's comedy and isn't featured here, then you're trying too hard. You should just relax and experience all this here funny stuff. This site is really easy to navigate, with the main links and a description of what to expect there running up and down the centre of the homepage. Once you're in a new section, the links are across the bottom of the page and up the left-hand side, so you can always get around without too much scrolling or use of the back button. It's also a fairly attractive site that has enough design not to be boring and not enough to be overly showy. Each of the main links takes you to detailed lists of links to explore. One nice touch is that the lists are not presented the same for each section, some thought has gone into making the site as interesting as possible. The site is frequently updated and every six months it gets a revamp.

SPECIAL FEATURES

Film and TV Comedy A great feature here allows you to click any year since 1960 and get a page dedicated to the period. There are historical facts and links to the top movies, as well as links to the top TV comedies of the year. The links take you to other sites outside the Comedy Zone. There are also links to classic comedy films and TV programmes.

Stand-up Comedy Click the initial letter of a performer to find them in the fairly comprehensive list.

overall rating: ★★★★★
classification: portal
updated: frequently
navigation: ★★★★★
content: ★★★★★
readability: ★★★★
speed: ★★★★★
UK

comedy

The Joke Files Over a thousand gags in 16 categories, with some adult content.

Comedy Directory Whatever you're looking for in the world of comedy, there will be a link to it here. Cartoons, Festivals, Cards, Satire, Street Entertainers, you name it, it's here.

OTHER FEATURES

There are more links to cartoon comedy, masses of trivia and hundreds of quotes in categories ranging from famous comedians' stand-up lines to daft political comments.

Superb place to find anything funny you can think of.

http://www.humorlinks.com
HumorLinks

overall rating:
★ ★ ★ ★ ★

classification:
links

updated:
daily

navigation:
★ ★ ★ ★ ★

content:
★ ★ ★ ★ ★

readability:
★ ★ ★ ★ ★

speed:
★ ★ ★ ★ ★

US

You can tell by the ridiculous misspelling of 'color' that this is not an English site but one of those created by American types . However, they think big, and this site is huge, massive, enormous and not small. There are 40 categories of links to be going along with. Including subsections, you are faced with a huge pile of links, 3215 at the last count, and growing. How do you know if a site is worth visiting? Well, each site listing, as well as having a brief description, has a star rating from one to five, voted for by people like you. Each link also tells you how often a site has been visited a month. Some of the most popular ones have links right at the top of the homepage. With all that choice at your disposal, if you can't find something you want, you may as well turn your monitor into a fish tank and admit your sense of humour has packed and left the building.

SPECIAL FEATURES

Hop To Two drop-down boxes make navigation easy. The one at the top of the page lists the categories and lets you do a key word search. The one at the bottom of the page lists sub-categories, which is useful if you know what you're looking for.

Very extensive lists of comedy sites, growing all the time. If you averaged out size, content and design, this site would probably be the best comedy link site on the internet.

comedy

overall rating: ★★★★★	
classification: links	
updated: infrequently	
navigation: ★★★★★	
content: ★★★★★	
readability: ★★★★	
speed: ★★★★★	

http://www.jokefairy.com/amusements/alphalist.php
Joke Fairy Links

If you are looking for sites dedicated to your favourite comedians, television shows or film, this is not the place for you. If you believe in the beautiful order of nature, righteousness and a society that seeks to improve itself by working intelligently and sensibly towards making the world a better place...then don't bother to pack, just run out of your house screaming and crying. These sites prove that your brave new world is over, and nonsensical anarchy reigns.

It looks like such a boring page, with the letters of the alphabet lined up innocently waiting to be clicked. But behind each letter are dozens of links to some of the world's most funny, stupid, and hysterically infantile places, and not necessarily in that order. It doesn't matter how often these lists are updated because your brain will shortly be frazzled by the content and you'll forget how to access your computer.

Think that's an exaggeration? Ok, click B and check out titles like Belly Button Walk of Fame, Build Your Own Cow, and Bureau of Missing Socks. Then click T for Three Kids Kicking the Crap Out of a Chair for No Particular Reason. Does anything more need to be said? Exactly. Updated now and then, whenever suitable stuff comes along.

Some sites may contain material unsuitable for children.

SPECIAL FEATURES
Random Link The only feature and, you guessed it, it gives you a link at random. At least then you can't be held responsible for the nonsense you're looking at.

Although the Joke Fairy site is covered elsewhere in this guide, its collection of links is so immense that it's well worthy of this individual entry.

comedy

overall rating: ★ ★ ★ ★ ★	

classification: guide	

updated: frequently	

navigation: ★ ★ ★ ★ ★	

content: ★ ★ ★ ★ ★	

readability: ★ ★ ★ ★ ★	

speed: ★ ★ ★ ★ ★	

UK

http://www.comedystar.com/index.cfm
The Comedy Star

Not to be mistaken for The Comedy Store, this site is a guide to all things involving performed comedy. So, there are no jokes, no games, no silly pictures and no crazy animations to download. Instead, you'll find articles about funny, professional comedy people and the professional comedy things they do, all packaged together like a glossy magazine. The site is rather hip, cool and trendy, with masses of information that is very easy to get around. The main links run down the left of the page, click these to get into the area you want. Each section has a main news story and a couple of links on the right to other relevant stories of the moment. There are also three more general links on the right-hand side of the page. Pretty frequently updated.

SPECIAL FEATURES

Stand-Up You can find out who's playing near you and read some of the up-to-the-minute news about stand-up comedians.

Theatre An often ignored section of the comedy world. Find out about comedy productions and comedy people who are taking to the boards.

Television Recent articles included Richard Wilson's thoughts on the demise of One Foot In The Grave and The League of Gentlemen discussing their new TV tie-in book.

Radio What to look out for in the next few days and details of programmes in the making.

Film Much more than just reviews and gossip. Here you'll find meaty reports on all aspects of comedy cinema. Recently, the rights to Chaplin films and an accolade given to Terry Gilliam were featured.

Books Snippets from new books and details of who's going to be out and about signing copies, so you can meet them and make a fool of yourself.

Edinburgh Details of the festival, past and present.

Browse Choose Artist, Show or Venue from the drop-down box, then choose the first letter of what you're looking for; use the Christian names of people. Then choose from the list for a brief summary and additional links.

Keep in touch with all the latest breaking stories in every field of comedy. Snappily written, very varied and frequently updated.

comedy

overall rating: ★ ★ ★ ★	
classification: portal	
updated: frequently	
navigation: ★ ★ ★ ★ ★	
content: ★ ★ ★ ★	
readability: ★ ★ ★ ★ ★	
speed: ★ ★ ★ ★ ★	
UK	

http://www.funny.co.uk
Funny.co.uk

From the beginning you'll see that this great looking site is dedicated to keeping you in touch with all things comedy. Recent press stories are in the centre of the page. If you want all the news for the last month, simply click the link beneath these first headlines. As a portal, Funny.co.uk will appeal to everyone. The site doesn't give you any bias to what it thinks is funny, it just points you in the direction you might want to go. It's a nice, modern design with funky links on the left that crawl up and down the page as you scroll, so you're never without access to the rest of the site. It's also updated fairly frequently and has the Database and UK Comedy Acts coming soon, which promise to be important sections once they get off the ground. So the site experience is getting larger all the time.

SPECIAL FEATURES

Web Directory Twelve links take you to specially selected, sometimes excellent sites, from Books and Classic Sit-Coms to Jokes and Weird Stuff. If you know a site that should be added to these relatively short lists, send it in. They're more than happy to at least look at your suggestions.

Joke Book Lots of jokes in lots of categories. It's not an original feature but this is as good as any other site. If the jokes aren't funny enough for you, why not send in your favourites? There's a simple form at the bottom of the page.

Fun Stuff Sites are obsessed with having a section like this, even if they don't really have anything to put in it. The only item of note is an Escape From The Wombles Of Hell game, which sounds pretty good but just turns out to be a text adventure where you make decisions by clicking links. It's not terribly eye-catching or thrilling.

Another well-designed starting place for your laughter needs.

comedy

overall rating: ★★★	
classification: links	
updated: occasionally	
navigation: ★★★★	
content: ★★★	
readability: ★★★★	
speed: ★★★★	
UK	

http://www.go2net.com/useless
The Useless Pages

You know what it's like, you're kicking around the web, not really sure what you're looking for, so many people are so dedicated to so many things and none of it really interests you. It's all so worthless and yet not worthless enough to spark life back into your weary surfing. Well, firstly, if you're thinking like that then you're not using this book properly. Secondly, help is at hand in the guise of this wonderful collection of sites dedicated to some of the stupidest things in the world. The site has links covering Uselessness from Elvis, Star Wars and Pets to Cows, Wackos and the painfully anal Homonymophone Debates. This stuff is so worthless and useless it will instantly give your life meaning and make the world a better place.

A list of assorted articles appears in the panel situated in the centre of the page. Other, more general topics are in the blue boxes to the right-hand side of the page, under the titles in the Uselessness Of ... , and More Useless Stuff.

SPECIAL FEATURES

Hack Your Big Mouth Billy Bass tells you how to hack into the Billy Bass microchip and customise the annoying novelty. Not exactly amusing reading, but if you have a degree in computer engineering, you could prolong the amusement value of your singing fish. Why would anyone bother? Why would they buy a Billy Bass in the first place?

The Uselessness of Computers contains links to sites computer-related, and, of course, utterly useless. In Available Domain names you'll find those 'wacky' domain names, which are still available to register. Sadly, dotcomfailure.com is not among them – some bright spark registered it in January. You can also view some of the least eligible bachelors on the web, in Who Wants to Marry a System Admin? Who Indeed?

The Uselessness of Elvis contains a plethora of links to all manner of bizarre Elvis sites, such as El Vez, the Spanish Elvis, and Elvis /Jesus similarities, which includes such gems as 'Jesus fasted for 40 days and nights, Elvis had irregular eating habits.'

The Uselessness of Spam includes links to the Monty Python Spam Sketch, Spam Carving Contests and Find the Spam.

The Uselessness of Wackos contains the quote 'When they say open mind, they mean brain removed with an ice cream scoop.' Need I say more?

OTHER FEATURES

The Uselessness of Domain Names, Fortune Telling and Parody Products, Machinery and Languages to name but a few.

Plenty that's mildly amusing, with the occasional gem.

OTHER SITES OF INTEREST

Frank Rapp's Humour Mailing Lists
http://www.angelfire.com/pa/humorlists/index.html

You don't want to spend hours and hours trudging around the internet, looking for humour, becoming depressed, do you? Of course not. That's why the nice Frank Rapp has collected together nearly 400 links to mailing lists, so you can have the jokes and silliness sent to your inbox without you having to do another thing. The quality of the links is extremely subjective, so click on a title and get a very brief idea of what to expect before you subscribe. Then sit back and wait for your computer to overflow with more nonsense than you can shake a pig at.

Newsgroups Available Under alt.comedy
http://cmc.qub.ac.uk/newslist/pages/alt.comedy.html

Not really a site in its own right, but rather part of a bigger site that lists comedy newsgroups. The ones listed are not the only comedy mailing lists in the world, but there are some pretty well known comedy subjects covered, and these lists are a great place to find more newsgroups. Just ask online. The list is especially good for those who have a particular interest in older comedy. There are lists for Laurel and Hardy, The Marx Brothers, Vaudeville and the Three Stooges, among others.

Top 50 JokeSites
http://www.bikinis98.com/cgi-bin/topsites/topsites.html

There are lots of sites that claim to list the 'Top' sites. This site even has a link to The Top 100 Humour Sites List. The link is included not to applaud it as a great site but to ask the question:

'Says Who?' It appears that, simply by sending in the name of your site, you have the chance of getting it included. The placing on the chart is decided by how many people visited your site over a period of time. That is not to say that the sites are not good, just that you should keep an open mind when a site offers you links to 'The Best' of anything. A lot of these sites feature material that is only suitable for adults.

for sale

If you're looking for comedy-related videos, books or CDs, there are dozens of large online stores just jumping up and down and dying to get you to part with your money. Most of them are not exclusively humour shops, just general retailers. What follows is a handful of places where you can go if you're looking for something a little different from the norm. You might find something for that annoying friend who is impossible to buy for. Because what do you buy the person who has everything? Something stupid? Exactly.

http://www.humorlinks.com/humornet/files/store.htm
HumorLinks

HumorLinks have taken a lot of the effort out of searching the net to look for humour sites. Although not exhaustive, they have a lot of good links, which are organised into easy-to-find sections. New stuff is added as it becomes available. This page is the Store, as they call it, which is a link to Amazon, but it will only give you the related comedy items so you get some great recommendations without the need to search. The only links you need to be concerned with are the three in the middle of the front page. And, unless you particularly want to look at the American or German versions of the store, a simple click on UK Store will take you where you want to go. It's very easy to get around and, with Amazon providing the goods, you can buy securely from one of the world's biggest online retailers. Although the site is based in America, all your orders from the UK store go through Amazon.co.uk, so they arrive much quicker.

overall rating:	★ ★ ★ ★ ★
classification:	e-commerce
updated:	regularly
navigation:	★ ★ ★ ★ ★
content:	★ ★ ★ ★
readability:	★ ★ ★ ★ ★
speed:	★ ★ ★ ★ ★
US	

SPECIAL FEATURES

UK Videos Chances are you already know what you're looking for. If so, simply click on the title of the video and you are immediately given details of the item, and very often, its healthy discount. If you're not looking for something definite and are more in the mood to browse, there's a great selection to choose from. There are videos old and new, ranging from Eric Sykes to

Red Dwarf and more. Clicking on film titles will take you directly to the film, situation comedies takes you to collections from the series, and clicking on a comedian's name will deliver a list of their videos, ranging from live shows and TV programmes to any films they've done. And don't forget, if you don't find exactly what you want, there is a search facility which should sort you out.

UK Books You'll find many of the same comedies and comedians listed here that were covered in the video section. You'll be amazed at how many books, scripts, tie-ins and audio books there are available. Once again, many of them have reductions, and if the book you want is currently unavailable, you can order it and they'll let you know when it comes in.

UK Music This is a little misleading as none of the comedy names you can click have made a record; you are simply told that no exact matches could be found. Unless you've changed your mind about buying something funny and decided to get some music instead, don't bother clicking this link.

Great for helping you come up with ideas, it's well organised and caters for comedic preferences.

http://www.sillyjokes.co.uk/index.html
Silly Jokes.co.uk

overall rating:
★ ★ ★ ★ ★

classification:
e-commerce

updated:
regularly

navigation:
★ ★ ★ ★

content:
★ ★ ★ ★ ★

readability:
★ ★ ★ ★ ★

speed:
★ ★ ★ ★ ★

UK

Some especially silly stuff for you to buy and amaze your friends with. The front page has that 'notice board' feel to it, as the site tries to tempt you to click on all manner of different products. If you'd prefer an overview of what's on offer, click the Site Map link under the Menu heading on the left of the front page to see the different sections. This is a well-constructed site; it's fairly plain, but the emphasis is on the products rather than design, so you won't mind too much. What is especially nice is that the site makes your visit fun rather than just trying to get you to part with your cash. There are all sorts of funny things to play and click around for each product, and as the site is constantly updated, there's always something new. Even if you don't buy anything, you'll still have a good time. And if you'd rather browse in your own time, they'll even send you a catalogue. Simply click on the Brochure link and fill out the form.

SPECIAL FEATURES

Billy Bob Teeth Outrageously realistic sets of comedy teeth. These are not the pathetic plastic things that fool no one; they're made of the same acrylic that real false teeth are made of. As well as Billy Bobs, there are also Austin Powers, Vampire and assorted other choppers. Take a trip to the Billy Bob Gallery, where you can see normal – well, nearly normal – people wearing the teeth.

comedy

Big Mouth Billy Bass This fish has been taking the country by storm, popping up all over the place. He flaps his tail to music and then surprises you by turning out front and singing certain lines right at you. If this doesn't make you laugh, you may be dead. Quite pricey, but worth every penny. You can hear his songs, watch him in action and even follow a link to details of how he works.

The Fart Machine You know you shouldn't find it funny, but once you've listened to some of the lifelike noises, you'll be smiling. You can't help it. And if you can't think what on earth a person could want such a farty machine for, there are even some suggestions as to where you can squeeze the maximum comedy value out of the odd windy pop. Listen to the sounds on offer, read the Fart Dictionary, read about Famous Farters, or even enjoy the odd fart joke. Infantile? Don't be absurd.

Weenie Beenies They're rude and you don't want your Gran to see them, but as hilarious comedy gifts go, they're excellent. What's more, they're not available anywhere else in the UK.

Fun Pages If you can't decide if you want to buy anything, why not take some time to think while you take a wander around these daft pages? Play the stupidly addictive Arse Race, watch silly animation or even play the old playground game Scissors, Paper, Stone.

OTHER FEATURES

The Essentials All the usual bits and pieces. Bookmark the site here, tell a friend, contact addresses and even a clever reminder service that sends you emails when birthdays or other important dates are approaching, so that you can pop over to the site and buy silly presents for people.

Wacky Products A variety of silly gifts, from fighting nuns and rubber chickens to the ridiculous Butt Head game and fake, but realistic, dog poo. You just know your life will be unfulfilled until you buy some of this stuff.

Thank heavens for this site. It's got everything that the proverbial person who's got everything hasn't got.

comedy

overall rating: ★ ★ ★ ★	
classification: e-commerce	
updated: frequently	
navigation: ★ ★ ★	
content: ★ ★ ★ ★	
readability: ★ ★ ★ ★	
speed: ★ ★ ★ ★ ★	
US	

http://www.mcphee.com/index.html
Archie McPhee

You've seen so many wonderfully silly things as you've wandered around the web, and now you just have to buy something. You know you do. Not videos and CDs, which you can get anywhere, but some really daft stuff that you're almost ashamed to admit you like. And this is a fantastic place to start. Probably aimed more at the student-minded among us, but the site also caters for those people who have everything and are impossible to buy presents for. It's silly, it's daft, and unfortunately it's also American, which means they'll only ship outside the USA and Canada if you buy more than $50 worth of stuff. Then they slap on a handling charge too. But, if you browse around, you may well see your price total for the things you want getting closer and closer to that elusive figure. They obviously want you to stumble across items you never even thought of, so naturally the navigation is not the most helpful in the world. The best place to start is with the red links running down the left of the page. Firstly you'll come across seasonal items, depending on what time of the year it is (Valentine's Day, Hallowe'en, and so on). Scroll down a bit further and you'll find their best-selling items. Updated several times a week.

SPECIAL FEATURES

Nerd Essentials The link, however, is called Geek; not very helpful, but there you are. There are loads of stupid presents, ranging from a squeaky lap-top Buddha to a pair of pants which are big enough for two. You know you personally don't want anything from here, but you can buy some really unusual presents for other people.

McPhee Classics So this is where you get a rubber chicken from. And their famous voodoo doll, which looks like a sock. Not sure why these are 'classic', but what other section would you put your Pink Lawn Flamingos in? You know you have to have them.

The Big Index This is a list of everything they sell, without the sales pitch. If you want more details, click on the item code and you'll be taken to the gift's own page.

Loads of nonsense to buy, secure online ordering, but unfortunately more expensive to those outside the USA and Canada.

comedy

overall rating: ★ ★ ★ ★	
classification: homepage	
updated: occasionally	
navigation: ★ ★ ★ ★ ★	
content: ★ ★ ★ ★	
readability: ★ ★ ★ ★	
speed: ★ ★ ★ ★ ★	
UK	

http://www.celebritycaricatures.com/html/start.html
CelebrityCaricatures.com

Every year birthdays come around, Christmas appears without warning and Special Occasions occur every other week. You've already bought everything in the world for every one of your family and friends. You need something new, and this site might just be able to provide it for you. Caricatures of the rich and famous, delivered to your door. All the caricatures are full colour and a perfect size for framing. There are quite a lot to choose from and a voting system helps to decide who will be next for the caricature treatment. And if your personal favourite is nowhere to be seen, there's a place to send in your own suggestions. The site is updated every few months and you can join the mailing list to find out what's been going on. To get around the site, click on the links on the left under the four main headings.

SPECIAL FEATURES

Caricatures The bulk of the site is here, with drawings split into categories. TV, Music, Movies and Other. You used to be able to get custom caricatures but this has stopped for the time being. You can also send an email postcard from here and download some of the images to use as wallpaper on your desktop.

Order Print If you want to buy something you don't buy online, so there are no worries about security. Simply fill out the form and the artist will be in touch with details of cost and how long you'll have to wait. Filling out the form places you under no obligation to actually buy.

OTHER FEATURES

Links Some of the artist's recommended sites.

Contact Me Join the mailing list, sign the guest book or drop the artist a line.

Well-drawn caricatures of familiar faces at reasonable prices. Great, original presents from a useful, nicely put together site.

comedy

overall rating: ★ ★ ★ ★	
classification: e-commerce	
updated: daily	
navigation: ★ ★ ★ ★	
content: ★ ★ ★ ★	
readability: ★ ★ ★ ★	
speed: ★ ★ ★ ★ ★	

http://www.ebay.co.uk
EBay.co.uk

'The World's Online Marketplace' is obviously not exclusively a comedy and humour auction site, but you can get such a lot of unusual things that if you're looking for something specific, it's a great place to start, as well as get a bargain. This is the UK version of the enormous American site, and though it's not as extensive it is good, nonetheless. The front page looks untidy, with lots of different features competing for your attention. For comedy-related items, go straight to the search facility at the top. To get the most out of the site you'll need to register, but it's quick and free.

SPECIAL FEATURES
For convenience, you might only want to look at items located in the UK. However, using this criterion when searching for 'comedy' only returned 37 hits. Clicking on the 'items available to the UK' got 1,372 hits. Sellers sometimes insist you pay in their home currency, and if you find something you really want, it's not such a chore.

Collectables A good place to look if you just fancy a browse. Looking through Animation Characters, Autographs, and Comic Books might turn up something you fancy.

A big site that's growing all the time. If you're looking for something unusual, be patient and prepared to browse.

http://www.cartooncharacters.sageweb.co.uk
CartoonCharacters.co.uk

Although their stock is limited to only four 'cartoons', they do happen to be four of the most successful animation productions ever: Wallace & Gromit, Chicken Run, South Park and The Simpsons. At least, that's what they'll be supplying online when they add the latter two which are 'coming soon'. So, for the time being, if you're not after Nick Park's creations, you're going to be disappointed. However, to get to the production you're interested in, click the icons at the top of the page and you're right there. The site is a little bit on the shabby side, with the graphics not as crystal clear as they might be, but it's the merchandise that you're interested in and there's plenty of that.

SPECIAL FEATURES

Wallace and Gromit You can choose from a selection of T-shirts, Mousemats, Watches, Clocks, Duvets and Plushies (which are character rucksacks). Each item has a little picture so you can see what you're getting. Annoyingly, a number of items are no longer available but the pictures are still there to tease you.

Chicken Run A slightly bigger selection to choose from, including some talking beanies, outrageous golf club covers, a wonderful talking money box, and an excellent looking radio.

Good news for fans of Wallace and Gromit and Chicken Run, but it needs to get on and deliver the content it promises.

overall rating:	★ ★ ★
classification:	e-commerce
updated:	infrequently
navigation:	★ ★ ★ ★ ★
content:	★ ★ ★
readability:	★ ★ ★ ★ ★
speed:	★ ★ ★ ★
UK	

OTHER SITES OF INTEREST

Amazon.co.uk

www.amazon.co.uk

If you've ever wanted to buy anything at all on the internet, you've almost certainly looked at this site. Amazon is one of the best places to buy books, CDs, videos and more. Just browse the area that interests you and buy securely online, or maybe try and pick up a bargain in the Auctions. Register and have special recommendations waiting for you every time you log on. They have also introduced a Wish List, which lets you specify items you would like to have; then, when your birthday or Christmas is coming around, simply point friends and family at this list and you'll hopefully get the presents you wanted.

Kelkoo

http://uk.kelkoo.com

There are so many places online trying to sell you things, how can you ever be sure you're getting the best possible bargain? Well, you can use a site like Kelkoo when shopping for your comedy videos and recordings, and lots more besides. First, click the section you're most interested in, be it Books, Toys, Gifts or one of their other sections. Then, on the next page, fill in as little or as much information as you have about the item then press Go to start the search. What Kelkoo does is search a number of online shops to see if they're selling the product you're after. Then it gives you all the results, so you can buy from the cheapest place. Very simple but quite brilliant, and utterly essential for all online purchases.

index